GOD BUILDS HIS CHURCH

THE STORY BIBLE SERIES

1. *God's Family* tells the story of creation, God's promises to Abraham's family, and the adventures of Joseph.

2. *God Rescues His People* tells about Israel's escape from Egypt, Moses and the Ten Commandments, and the wandering in the wilderness.

3. *God Gives the Land* tells the story of Joshua, the adventures of the judges, and the story of Ruth.

4. *God's Chosen King* tells about Samuel, Saul, and David, God's promises to David's family, and the Psalms.

5. *God's Wisdom and Power* tells about the glorious reign of Solomon, the wonderful works of Elijah and Elisha, and the Proverbs and the Song of Songs.

6. *God's Justice* tells the story of the prophets Amos, Hosea, Isaiah, and Jeremiah and their messages of God's judgment and mercy.

7. *God Comforts His People* tells about God's people in exile, their return to Judah, and the adventures of Esther and Daniel.

8. *God Sends His Son* tells about God sending Jesus to set up his kingdom.

9. *God's Suffering Servant* tells about the last week of Jesus' life, his suffering, death, and resurrection.

10. *God Builds His Church* tells about the coming of the Holy Spirit, the adventures of the apostles, and John's vision of the end of the world.

Story Bible Series, Book 10

GOD BUILDS HIS CHURCH

Stories of God and His People from Acts, Galatians, 1 and 2 Thessalonians, 1 and 2 Corinthians, Romans, Philippians, Colossians, Ephesians, Philemon, 1 and 2 Timothy, Titus, Hebrews, Jude, James, 1 and 2 Peter, 1, 2, and 3 John, and Revelation

Retold by Eve B. MacMaster
Illustrated by James Converse

HERALD PRESS
Scottdale, Pennsylvania
Kitchener, Ontario
1987

Library of Congress Cataloging-in-Publication Data

MacMaster, Eve, 1942-
  God builds His church.

  (Story Bible series ; bk. 10)
  Summary: Retells the book of Acts, includes brief
summaries from the Epistles, and concludes with major
sections from Revelation.
  1. Bible stories, English—N.T. Acts. 2. Bible
stories, English—N.T. Epistles of Paul. 3. Bible
stories, English—N.T. Revelation. [1. Bible stories—
N.T.] I. Converse, James, ill. II. Title. III. Series.
BS2617.8.M33 1987   225.9'505   87-2875
ISBN 0-8361-3446-X (soft)

GOD BUILDS HIS CHURCH
Copyright © 1987 by Herald Press, Scottdale, Pa. 15683
    Published simultaneously in Canada by Herald Press,
    Kitchener, Ont. N2G 4M5. All rights reserved.
Library of Congress Catalog Card Number: 87-2875
International Standard Book Number: 0-8361-3446-X
Printed in the United States of America

93 92 91 90 89 88 87 10 9 8 7 6 5 4 3 2 1

The Story of This Book

Several years ago I was looking for a Bible story book to read to my children. I wanted one that was complete, without tacked-on morals or a denominational interpretation. I wanted one that was faithful to the Bible and fun to read. I couldn't find what I was looking for.

With the encouragement of my husband, Richard MacMaster, I approached Herald Press with the idea of the series: a retelling of the whole Bible with nothing added and nothing subtracted, just following the story line through the Old and New Testaments.

The people at Herald Press were agreeable and enthusiastic and gave much valuable advice, especially general book editor Paul M. Schrock.

At his suggestion, I asked some academic and professional people in our community to check the stories for style and accuracy. Members of the advisory committee, who have kindly volunteered their time, include Bible professors George R. Brunk III, Ronald D. Guengerich, G. Irvin Lehman, and Kenneth Seitz; and childhood curriculum and librarian specialists Elsie E. Lehman and A. Arlene Bumbaugh.

I hope this series will lead its readers to the original, for no retelling is a substitute for the Bible itself. The Bible is actually a collection of books written over a long period of time in a variety of forms. It has been translated and retold in every generation because people everywhere want to know what God is like.

The main character in every story is God. The plot of every story is God's activity among his people: creating, saving, fighting, reigning, and doing works of wisdom and power, justice and mercy.

The first book in the series is *God's Family*. It tells stories about God the Creator.

The second book is *God Rescues His People*. It tells stories about God the Savior.

The third book is *God Gives the Land*. It tells stories about God the warrior.

The fourth book, *God's Chosen King*, tells stories about God the true King.

The fifth book, *God's Wisdom and Power*, tells stories about God, the source of wisdom and power.

The sixth book, *God's Justice*, tells stories about God the righteous Judge.

The seventh book, *God Comforts His People*, tells stories about God's comforting mercy and promises.

The eighth book, *God Sends His Son*, tells about Jesus the teacher and miracle-worker.

The ninth book, *God's Suffering Servant*, tells about Jesus the humble servant and sacrificial lamb.

This book, *God Builds His Church*, tells stories about the Holy Spirit, who works through the apostles to spread the good news about the kingdom of God.

This volume is dedicated to the church of Jesus Christ, especially the fellowships of St. Luke's, Washington, D.C.; St. David's, Cullowhee, N.C.; Park View, and Asbury, Harrisonburg, Va.

—Eve MacMaster
Bluffton, Ohio
Christmas, 1986

Contents

God Makes All Things New

Maps

The Coming
of the Holy Spirit

Jesus Is Taken Up to Heaven

Acts 1

JESUS is alive!"

"He has risen from the dead!"

"We've seen him!"

Jesus' friends told the good news over and over. They knew he was really alive, because they had seen him. They were witnesses.

Jesus appeared to his followers for forty days, teaching them about the kingdom of God. Then on the fortieth day after he rose from the dead, he left them.

At the Mount of Olives, just outside Jerusalem,

Jesus met with his closest followers, the apostles. "Don't leave Jerusalem," he told them. "Wait for God to send the gift I've told you about. My Father has promised to send you the gift of the Holy Spirit. You have already been baptized with water. Soon you'll be baptized with the Holy Spirit!"

"Lord," said the apostles, "has the time come? Are you going to bring back the kingdom for Israel?"

His answer surprised them. Instead of speaking about a kingdom for Israel, Jesus spoke about God's rule spreading all over the world.

"It's not for you to know the future," said Jesus. "That's only for God to know. But when the Holy Spirit comes, you'll be filled with power. And with the power of the Holy Spirit upon you, you will be witnesses to me—in Jerusalem, all over Judea and Samaria, and even to the ends of the earth!"

As he was saying this, Jesus was taken up to heaven right in front of them, and a cloud hid him from their eyes.

While they were standing there, staring up into the sky, two angels dressed in white suddenly stood beside them.

"Men of Galilee!" said the angels. "Why are you standing here looking up into the sky? This Jesus who was taken from you into heaven will come back the same way you saw him go."

So the apostles returned to Jerusalem, to the

upstairs room where they had been staying. There were eleven apostles now: Peter, John, James, Andrew, Philip, Thomas, Bartholomew, Matthew, James the son of Alpheus, Simon the patriot, and Judas the son of James. Judas Iscariot, the twelfth apostle, was dead. He had betrayed Jesus, and then he had died a horrible death.

Now the eleven apostles were meeting in the upper room to pray. With them were other people who had followed Jesus, including Jesus' mother, Mary, and his brothers.

One day while about a hundred and twenty of these believers were meeting together, Peter stood up and spoke to them.

"Friends," said Peter, "the prophecies in the Scriptures have come true. Jesus was betrayed by one of his friends, and now that man— Judas—is dead. Scripture also says that someone must take Judas' place. It must be someone who has been with us the whole time that the Lord Jesus was with us, from the time John the Baptist baptized him until the day he was taken up to heaven. It must be someone who was an eyewitness with us, someone who saw the Lord Jesus after his resurrection from the dead."

Two names were suggested—Joseph Barsabbas and Matthias. Then the believers prayed for God's help.

"Lord," they prayed, "you know everyone's thoughts. Show us which of these two men you have chosen to take Judas' place as the twelfth apostle."

They drew lots to choose between the two men, and Matthias was chosen. After that Matthias was counted as one of the twelve apostles.

The Coming of the Holy Spirit

Acts 2

THE Jews were celebrating the feast of Pentecost. This was the spring harvest festival, a time when the Jews thanked God for the first-fruits of the harvest. It was also a time when they celebrated the special agreement between God and his people called the covenant.

According to the covenant, the Lord promised to be their God, to take care of them, and to save them from their enemies. The people agreed to worship the Lord and obey his teachings.

This year on the day of Pentecost the twelve

15

apostles and other disciples of Jesus met together. It was just ten days since Jesus had gone up to heaven.

Suddenly they heard a sound from heaven like the rushing of a mighty wind. It filled the whole house where they were sitting. They saw something that looked like tongues of fire, which separated and rested above the head of each person.

They were all filled with the Holy Spirit, and they began to speak in foreign languages, as the Spirit gave them power.

At this time faithful Jews from many foreign countries were in Jerusalem for the feast of Pentecost. When they heard this sound, a large crowd of them gathered in front of the house where the disciples were meeting. They were amazed by the miracles they heard: the disciples were speaking foreign languages!

"Listen!" they said to each other with great excitement. "Surely these speakers are from Galilee! How is it possible that each of us hears them speaking in our native language? We come from many different countries: from the Parthian Empire and Mesopotamia in the east; from Judea and Asia Minor; from Egypt and North Africa and Rome in the west! Some of us were born Jews, and some of us have joined the Jewish faith. We're from places like Crete and Arabia—yet all of us can hear them speaking in our own languages about the wonders of God!"

They couldn't explain it. They were so surprised, they kept asking each other, "What does it mean?"

But some people in the crowd weren't impressed. They laughed and said, "These people are drunk! They've been drinking too much new wine!"

Peter and the other apostles stepped forward, and in a loud voice Peter began to speak to the crowd.

"People of Jerusalem and fellow Jews," he said, "listen carefully while I tell you what's happening. These people aren't drunk, as you suppose. After all, it's only nine o'clock in the morning! Something wonderful is happening. This is the miracle that the prophet Joel said would happen, when he wrote:

"The day will come," says the Lord,
"when I will pour out my Spirit
on all nations.

"Your sons and daughters will prophesy,
your young people will see visions,
and your old people will dream dreams.

"Yes, even on my servants, both men and women,
I will pour out my Spirit,
and they will preach my message."

"People of Israel!" said Peter. "Listen to me! Jesus of Nazareth was sent to you by God. He did great works among you through the power of God. God allowed you to put Jesus to death, for that was part of his plan. Then God raised Jesus to life. He saved him from the power of death!"

Peter showed them how the Scriptures told about Jesus. Jesus was the Messiah, the Christ that the prophets had spoken about. He was the king God had chosen to save his people.

"God has raised this man Jesus to life, and all of us are witnesses!" said Peter. "Now Jesus is in heaven with God the Father, and he has poured out the Holy Spirit on us. That's what you see and hear. Now you can know for sure that this Jesus whom you crucified is the one that God has made Lord and Christ!"

Many of the people believed the good news.

They believed that Jesus was the Christ, and they were sorry for their sins.

"What must we do, brothers?" they asked the apostles.

Peter answered, "You must turn from your sins. You must turn to God and be baptized in the name of Jesus Christ. Then your sins will be forgiven, and you will receive the gift of the Holy Spirit. For God's promise was made to you, to your children, and even to foreigners—to everyone the Lord our God chooses!"

Peter talked to them a long time, encouraging them to turn to God. "Let yourselves be saved from the punishment that's coming to the wicked!" he said.

Many of the people believed the message and were baptized. That day about three thousand people were added to the community of believers.

3

The Power
of Jesus' Name

Acts 2—3

WHEN they joined the community of believers, the new disciples spent their time learning from the apostles, worshiping God, and sharing the life of the community.

All the believers shared everything they owned. Some sold their belongings and their land and gave the money to the community, to be divided according to what each person needed. Every day they went to the temple for worship and met in their houses to eat together. They shared their food gladly and kept praising God.

All the people of Jerusalem respected them and every day the Lord added to the community more people who were being saved.

One afternoon Peter and John went to the temple to pray. At the gate called Beautiful they saw a man who had been crippled all his life. Every day this man was carried to the gate of the temple, so he could sit and beg as people were going in.

When he saw Peter and John going in to the temple, the man asked them to give him something.

Peter looked directly at him, and so did John. Then Peter said, "Look straight at us!"

The man looked at them, hoping they would give him some money.

"If you're expecting silver or gold," said Peter, "I have none. But what I do have, I will certainly give to you: *In the name of Jesus Christ of Nazareth, walk!*"

Then Peter took the man by the hand and helped him up.

Immediately his feet and ankles became strong. He jumped up and stood on his feet and began to walk around. He went with them into the temple, walking, leaping and praising God.

Everyone noticed the man as he walked around. They recognized him as the beggar who used to sit at the Beautiful Gate, and they were amazed by what had happened.

While the man was still hanging on to Peter

and John, the people came running. They crowded around them at the place called Solomon's Porch.

"People of Israel," said Peter to the crowd, "why are you so surprised? Why are you staring at us? Do you think we made this man walk by some power of our own? No, the God of our ancestors, the God of Abraham, Isaac, and Jacob did this. He did it to give glory to his servant, Jesus—the same Jesus you handed over to the Romans to be killed. You killed him, but God raised him from the dead. We are witnesses!"

Peter continued, "It is the power of Jesus' name that made this man well. It is faith in Jesus that healed him, as you all can see.

"Friends, I know that you and your leaders didn't realize what you were doing when you killed Jesus. But now you must turn to God, so your sins can be wiped out. If you do, God will be with you. Remember what God said to our ancestor, Abraham: 'All the nations of the world will receive my blessing through you and your family.' That's why God sent Jesus to the Jews first—to bring you great blessing by turning you from your sins."

Just then some priests and religious leaders arrived with the officer in charge of the temple police. They were angry at Peter and John for teaching the people that Jesus had risen from the dead. They arrested them and put them in jail for the night.

But many of the people who heard Peter and John's message became believers, and the number of disciples grew to five thousand.

The next day the leaders of the ruling council of the Jews met with Annas, the high priest, and other religious leaders. They had Peter and John brought in, and also the man who had been healed.

"How did you do this?" they demanded. "What power did you use? In whose name did you work this miracle?"

Peter, filled with the Holy Spirit, answered, "Leaders of the people, elders of Israel, if you want to know about the good thing that happened to this lame man, and how he was healed, then I'll be glad to tell you. I'd be glad to tell everyone!

"We worked this miracle in the name of Jesus Christ of Nazareth. He's the one you crucified. But God raised him from the dead. It is through his power, and no other, that this man can stand here today perfectly healthy. In all the world, no other name has been given by God except the name of Jesus Christ. It is by Jesus' name that we all are saved!"

The members of the council were astonished. How could Peter and John be so sure of themselves? They were ordinary men, with no education. They were simple fishermen from Galilee.

The wealthy and educated religious leaders didn't know what to do now. They didn't know what to say. After all, there was the man who had been healed, standing right next to Peter and John. They ordered the apostles to go outside while they talked privately.

"What can we do with these men?" they asked each other.

"Everyone in Jerusalem can see that a great miracle has been worked through them. We can't argue with that," one said.

"But we must stop this thing from spreading any further among the people. We must order them not to speak anymore in the name of Jesus," another replied.

Then they called Peter and John back in and ordered them never to speak or teach another word in the name of Jesus.

But Peter and John answered, "It's for you to judge whether it's right in God's sight for us to obey you or God. But as for us, we can't help speaking about what we have seen and heard!"

The council warned Peter and John again. They threatened to punish them if they spoke any more in the name of Jesus. Then they let them go. But Peter and John didn't see how they could do anything else, because the people were praising God for what had happened. (The man who had been healed was more than forty years old.)

As soon as they were free, Peter and John went back to their friends and told them what the council had done. When the believers heard their report, they joined together in prayer.

"Lord," they prayed, "you're the one who made heaven and earth and the sea, and everything in them. You knew these things would happen. It was part of your plan for your Christ to be killed by powerful men. Now, Lord, these same rulers are making threats against us. Please give us, your servants, the courage to speak your message boldly. Reach out your hand to heal, and let miracles be done through the name of your holy servant, Jesus."

As they prayed, the house they were meeting in began to shake. They were all filled with the Holy Spirit, and they preached God's message without fear.

4

The Sharing Community

Acts 4—5

THE apostles kept witnessing to Jesus with great power. They told the people of Jerusalem how Jesus had risen from the dead, and they worked many miracles.

A wonderful spirit of sharing filled the community of believers. The whole community was united in heart and mind. No one in the church was poor, because the rich people sold their land and their belongings and gave the money to the apostles to divide among the poor. They divided the money according to what each person needed.

No one said that any of their belongings were their own. Everything was common property and shared with the whole community.

At this time a disciple named Joseph sold some land and brought the money to the apostles. Joseph was a kind man, and the apostles nicknamed him Barnabas, meaning "one who encourages others."

But there was another man, Ananias, who did something wicked. Ananias and his wife, Sapphira, sold some land that belonged to them. But Ananias kept part of the money for himself, even though he said he was giving all of it to the apostles. Sapphira knew what he was doing.

"Ananias," said Peter, "why did you let Satan fill you and make you lie to the Holy Spirit? Why did you keep part of the money for yourself? No one forced you to share your property. Before you sold the land, it belonged to you. After you sold it, the money was yours to keep. But when you pretended to be sharing all of the money, you were lying. Why did you do such a thing? You haven't lied to humans. You have lied to God!"

As soon as Ananias heard this, he dropped dead. Everyone in the room was terrified. The young men stood up, wrapped the body in a sheet, and carried it out and buried it.

About three hours later Sapphira came in. She didn't know what had happened.

"Tell me," said Peter. "Was this what you and your husband received for your land?"

"Yes," she answered. "The full amount."

Then Peter said, "You and your husband agreed to put the Spirit of the Lord to the test! How could you do such a thing?"

He paused. "Do you hear those footsteps?" he asked. "They're the footsteps of the men who are coming back from burying your husband. They'll carry you out, too!"

Immediately, Sapphira fell down dead. The young men came into the room and found her there at Peter's feet, and they carried her out and buried her beside her husband.

A feeling of holy fear came over the whole church and everyone who heard about these things. When the believers met at Solomon's

Porch, other people were afraid to join them. Yet they were respected, and more and more people became believers.

5

Gamaliel's Good Advice

Acts 5

THE high priests and the religious leaders of Jerusalem were furious. Wherever they went, they heard about the miracles that the apostles were working.

People were bringing their sick friends out into the streets and laying them on mats, hoping that when Peter walked by, at least his shadow would fall on the sick people.

Crowds were coming into Jerusalem from the nearby towns, bringing sick people and persons with evil spirits, and they were all healed.

The religious leaders were so jealous of these miracles, they had the apostles arrested and thrown into jail.

But that night an angel of the Lord opened the prison gates and led the apostles out.

"Go stand in the temple," said the angel. "Tell the people all about this new life!"

The apostles did as the angel said. As soon as the sun came up, they went to the temple and began to speak.

Meanwhile, the high priest and the religious leaders called a meeting of the ruling council of the Jews. Then they sent for the apostles.

The temple police went to the jail, but they came back empty-handed.

"We found the jail locked up tight," they reported. "The guards were on duty at the gates. But when we went in, we couldn't find anyone!"

The officer in charge couldn't figure it out. The chief priests didn't know what to think.

Just then a messenger arrived. "Listen!" he said. "The men you put in jail are standing in the temple, teaching the people!"

The officer and police went out to arrest the apostles. They didn't dare use force, though, because they were afraid that the people might stone them. They took them quietly and brought them back to the council.

"We warned you!" the high priest said to the apostles. "We ordered you not to speak or teach in the name of that man Jesus! Now look what's happening! You've filled Jerusalem with your teaching. What's more, you're trying to blame us for his death."

Peter and the other apostles answered the high priest, saying, "We must obey God instead of people. The God of our ancestors raised Jesus up to be ruler and Savior, to bring a change of heart and forgiveness of sins to the people of Israel. We are witnesses to these things—we and the Holy Spirit, whom God gives to the people who obey him."

When the council heard this, they were so angry, they wanted to kill the apostles.

Then a religious teacher named Gamaliel stood up. Gamaliel was a highly respected rabbi. He asked the leaders to take the apostles outside for a few minutes, and then he gave the council some advice.

"Leaders of Israel!" he said. "Be very careful what you do to these people. Remember a while back when a man named Theudas appeared? He said he was the Christ. He became famous and gathered four hundred followers. He was killed, and his followers were scattered, and that was the end of it.

"After that there was Judas the Galilean, who appeared during the time of the census. Many people followed him, but he was killed, too, and his followers were scattered.

"So I tell you: leave these people alone. Don't do anything to them. If this movement of theirs

is only human, it will fall apart. But if it comes from God, you can't possibly defeat them—and you could find yourselves fighting against God!"

The council decided to follow Gamaliel's good advice. They called the apostles back in, had them beaten, and ordered them not to speak in the name of Jesus. Then they let them go.

The apostles left the council full of joy, because God had given them the honor of suffering for Jesus.

Day after day they kept teaching in the temple and in homes, telling everyone the good news about Jesus Christ.

6

Stephen, the First Christian Martyr

Acts 6—7

DURING the time when the Romans ruled the world, the Jews were scattered across the Roman Empire. They kept their own religion, but they spoke the languages of the empire. In the west they spoke Latin, and in the east they spoke Greek. The Jews who lived in Judea spoke Aramaic.

Both "Hebrew" Jews and "Greek" Jews lived in Jerusalem. Both became followers of Jesus. But as the number of believers grew, bad feelings also grew between the two groups. The Greek-speaking Jews complained to the apostles about the Hebrews. They said that their widows weren't being treated fairly. When food was passed out each day, the Hebrew widows received more than the Greek widows.

The apostles called the whole community together to settle this problem. "We shouldn't be doing this," they said. "We shouldn't have to stop preaching to settle community problems. Friends, this is something you must do yourselves. Choose seven men you respect, men filled with the Holy Spirit and wisdom. We'll put them in charge of this work. Then we'll be able to spend all our time praying and preaching."

Everyone agreed to follow the apostles' plan. They chose Stephen, a man full of faith and the Holy Spirit, Philip, and five other men. They took these seven to the apostles, and the apostles prayed and laid their hands on them. Laying on of hands was a sign that the seven were receiving the power of God to do the work of the church. The seven men were called "servers" or "deacons."

After the community solved this problem, the number of disciples in Jerusalem grew larger and larger. Many of the Jewish priests became believers.

At the same time, Stephen was so full of God's grace and power, he worked great miracles among the people.

Then some Jews from North Africa, Cilicia,

and Asia Minor began to work against Stephen. They argued with him, but they couldn't win, because the Holy Spirit gave Stephen wisdom for debating.

Stephen's enemies were so annoyed, they paid some men to lie about him. The liars said, "We heard this man speaking against Moses and God." This way they upset the religious leaders and the people and turned them against Stephen.

Then Stephen's enemies grabbed him and took him to the ruling council of the Jews. There they brought in more people to speak against him.

These witnesses lied and said, "This man is always talking against our temple and the law of Moses. We heard him say that Jesus of Nazareth will destroy the temple and change all the customs that Moses gave us."

The whole council sat there, staring at Stephen. His face looked to them like the face of an angel.

"Is this true?" asked the high priest.

"Men of Israel," answered Stephen, "listen to me!" He spoke to the council a long time, telling them about all the times their ancestors had rejected God's prophets. He reminded them how their ancestors had persecuted and killed God's messengers.

Then Stephen said, "You stubborn people! You're just like your ancestors! You refuse to listen to God's message. Was there a single prophet your ancestors didn't persecute? They

killed the messengers who told about the coming
of the Christ. And when Christ came, you killed
him. God has loved you and watched over you.
He has given you his law, his teachings. But you
have disobeyed him!"

Stephen's speech made the council so angry,
they ground their teeth in rage.

But Stephen was filled with the Holy Spirit.
He looked up to heaven and saw the glory of God
and Jesus himself standing at God's right hand.

"Look!" he cried. "The heavens are opened, and
I can see the Son of Man standing at the right
hand of God!"

When the council heard this, they put their fin-
gers over their ears. Screaming with rage, they

rushed at Stephen and dragged him out of the city to stone him to death.

They laid their cloaks at the feet of a young man named Saul. Then they threw stones at Stephen.

"Lord Jesus," prayed Stephen, "receive my spirit!" He kneeled down and called out, "Lord, forgive them for this sin."

With these words, Stephen died. He was the first Christian martyr, the first person to be killed for witnessing about Jesus.

7

Witnesses All Over Judea and Samaria

Acts 8

THE believers buried Stephen and mourned and cried for him. That same day the enemies of the church began to persecute them.

The leader of the persecution was the young man named Saul who had watched Stephen die. Saul was glad that Stephen was stoned to death, because he wanted to stop this movement. Saul was a member of the strictest group of religious teachers, the Pharisees. He thought the people who believed in Jesus should be wiped out, and he made up his mind to do it.

With the permission of the high priest, Saul went from house to house, dragging out the believers, both men and women, and throwing them into jail.

As a result of this persecution, everyone except the apostles left Jerusalem. The believers scattered over the countryside of Judea and Samaria, and as they went, they preached the good news about Jesus Christ.

One of the believers who escaped from Jerusalem was Philip, one of the seven deacons. Philip went to a city in Samaria and preached about Jesus to the people there. Large crowds listened to him and saw the miracles he worked, and they welcomed his message.

Many evil spirits came out of people, screaming as they left, and many paralyzed and crippled people were healed. Because of these miracles, great joy filled the city.

In that city lived a magician named Simon. Simon had impressed the Samaritans by practicing his magic and saying that he was a great man.

Everyone in the city listened to Simon. "He's a great man," they said. "He has the power of God."

This had been going on for a long time, but when Philip told the Samaritans about Jesus, they believed and were baptized. Even Simon the magician became a believer. After Simon was baptized, he stayed close to Philip, because he

40

was amazed by the great miracles that God was working through him.

When the apostles in Jerusalem heard that the Samaritans had accepted God's message, they sent Peter and John to Samaria. Peter and John came and prayed for the Samaritans to receive the Holy Spirit, which had not yet come on any of them. The Samaritans had only been baptized in the name of the Lord Jesus.

As Peter and John laid their hands on the Samaritans, they received the Holy Spirit. Simon saw this, and he offered money to Peter and John.

"Give me this power, too," he said, "so I can lay my hands on people and cause them to receive the Holy Spirit."

Peter answered, "May you and your money go to hell! How dare you think you can buy God's gift with money. You can't share in this work, because your heart isn't right in God's sight. Turn from this wickedness! Pray to God to forgive you for thinking such a thing. I can see that you're bitter with jealousy and trapped in your sin!"

"Please!" answered Simon. "Pray to the Lord for me, so none of these things happen."

Then Peter and John finished giving their witness and preaching God's message in that city, and they went back to Jerusalem. On the way, they shared the gospel in many Samaritan villages.

Philip also left the city. An angel of the Lord

said to him, "Get up and go down the road to Gaza, through the desert."

Philip got up and went where the angel said. At the same time, a man who was the treasurer of the queen of Ethiopia was traveling on that same road.

This important official was on his way home from Jerusalem, where he had gone to worship God at the temple. As he was riding in his carriage, he was reading from the Scriptures, from the book of Isaiah.

Then the Holy Spirit said to Philip, "Go over to that carriage and keep close to it."

When Philip went over to the carriage, he heard the man reading out loud to himself.

"Do you understand what you're reading?" asked Philip.

"How can I," answered the man, "unless I have someone to guide me?"

Then he invited Philip to get into the carriage and sit beside him.

This is what he was reading from the prophet Isaiah:

> He was led like a sheep to be butchered,
> like a lamb when its wool is cut off.
>
> He said nothing;
> he didn't open his mouth.
>
> When he was insulted,
> no one spoke up for him.
>
> He'll have no children to speak about,
> for his life has been cut off short.

"Tell me, please," asked the man. "Who is the prophet talking about? Himself or someone else?"

Then Philip told the Ethiopian official the good news about Jesus. Beginning with the prophecy of Isaiah, he explained how Jesus came to suffer and die, and how Jesus brings new life to everyone who believes in him.

They traveled on down the road together, with Philip sharing the gospel and the man listening eagerly. When they came to some water, the man said, "Look! Here's some water. Is there any reason I can't be baptized now?"

He gave orders for the carriage to stop, and he and Philip went down to the water. There Philip baptized him.

When they came up out of the water, the Spirit of the Lord suddenly took Philip away. The Ethiopian official didn't see Philip anymore, but he went on his way with his heart full of joy.

Philip was taken by the Spirit of the Lord to the town of Azotus, and from there he traveled north to the city of Caesarea. As he went through the countryside, he preached the gospel in every town.

8

God Chooses Saul

Acts 9, 22, 26; Galatians 1; 2 Corinthians 11; Philippians 3

THE believers preached the gospel everywhere they went, and the church spread all over Judea and Samaria. But Saul kept trying to destroy the church. He went to the synagogues, where the Jews met for worship. There he found many followers of Jesus, and he tried to force them to give up their faith. With the help of the chief priests, Saul had many believers arrested.

When the believers ran away to foreign cities, Saul followed them. He hated them so much, he wanted to kill them.

Then Saul asked the high priest to write letters for him to take to the synagogues in Damascus, letters giving him permission to go to Damascus and arrest the believers and bring them back to Jerusalem.

When he received the papers from the high priest, Saul left for Damascus, along with some men to help him find and arrest the believers. About the middle of the day, as Saul was coming near Damascus, something strange and wonderful happened.

A bright light suddenly flashed around him, and he fell to the ground. He heard a voice speaking to him.

"Saul! Saul!" said the voice. "Why are you persecuting me?"

"Who are you, Lord?" asked Saul.

The voice answered, "I am Jesus of Nazareth, whom you are persecuting."

"What should I do, Lord?" asked Saul.

The Lord answered, "Stand up and go into the city. There you will be told what you must do."

The men traveling with Saul didn't know what was going on. They just stood there, unable to speak.

Saul stood up and opened his eyes. He was blinded by the light from heaven, so they took him by the hand and led him into the city. There he stayed, unable to see, for three days. During that time he didn't eat any food or drink any water.

Meanwhile, the Lord was speaking to a disciple named Ananias, who lived in Damascus.

"Ananias!" he said in a vision.

"Here I am, Lord," answered Ananias.

The Lord said, "Get up and go down to the street called Straight. At the house of Judas ask for a man named Saul from Tarsus. At this very moment Saul is praying and seeing a vision of you coming in and laying hands on him, to give him back his sight."

"Lord!" said Ananias. "I've heard about this man Saul. He's been doing terrible things to your saints in Jerusalem! Now he has come to Damascus with papers from the chief priests, so he can arrest everyone who calls on your name."

"You must go to Saul," the Lord said to Ananias. "I have chosen him to serve me. He will take my name to other nations and their rulers, as well as to the people of Israel. And I will show him what he must suffer for my sake."

Then Ananias went to the street called Straight, to the house of Judas, where Saul was staying. He went in and laid hands on Saul and said to him, "Brother Saul, the Lord has sent me—Jesus himself, who appeared to you on your way here. He sent me to lay hands on you, so you may see again, and so you may be filled with the Holy Spirit."

Immediately, Saul's eyes were opened and he could see again.

Then Ananias said to him, "The God of our ancestors has chosen you. Jesus himself will appear to you and speak to you. You will be his witness to the ends of the earth. Now, what are you waiting for? Get up and be baptized! Have your sins washed away as you call on the name of Jesus!"

Saul got up, and Ananias baptized him. Then he ate some food and felt strong again.

Saul stayed with the believers in Damascus for a while, and he went to the synagogues and preached that Jesus was the Son of God.

The people in the synagogues were shocked. "This is the man who led the persecution in Jerusalem," they said. "He hated the followers of Jesus! Why, he came here to Damascus just so he could arrest them and take them back as prisoners to the chief priests!"

Saul kept on preaching, and his preaching became more powerful. He proved that Jesus was the Messiah, and the Jews of Damascus couldn't answer him.

Saul spent some time in the desert south of Damascus, and then he returned to the city. About three years after he became a believer, his enemies began to plot against him. They made plans to kill him. They watched the city gates day and night, trying to catch him, but Saul was able to escape.

The believers found out about the plot and told Saul. They had him climb through a window, and then they lowered him down the side of the city wall in a basket. In this unusual and undignified way, he sneaked out of the city.

Then Saul went to Jerusalem, where he wanted to see the disciples. But they were afraid of him, because they thought it was impossible for Saul the persecutor to be a believer.

Then Barnabas, the man who had sold some land and given the money to the church, took Saul by the hand and introduced him to Peter and James, the brother of the Lord. He told them how Saul had seen the Lord on the road to Damascus and how the Lord had spoken to him. He told them that Saul had witnessed boldly in Damascus.

After that, Saul joined the disciples and

preached boldly in Jerusalem. He argued with the Greek-speaking Jews, trying to convince them that Jesus was the Messiah.

One day while Saul was praying in the temple in Jerusalem, he saw a vision of the Lord.

"Hurry!" said the Lord. "Leave Jerusalem right now, for the people here won't listen to your preaching."

"But Lord," said Saul. "They know how I tried to persecute the church. I even helped the men who killed Stephen."

"You must leave," said the Lord. "I'm going to send you to nations far away from here."

Saul left Jerusalem right away. He traveled overland to Caesarea, and then by sea to Tarsus, his hometown, in the province of Cilicia. He spent the next ten years in Cilicia and Syria.

During this time most of the believers didn't know Saul, but they heard about him. They heard that the man who had persecuted them was now preaching the faith he had tried to destroy. And when they heard, they thanked God for what had happened.

9

The Story of Peter and Cornelius

Acts 9—11

WHEN Saul stopped persecuting the church, the believers were left in peace. For the next few years, with the help of the Holy Spirit, the number of believers grew, and their faith became stronger.

Peter helped build up the church by traveling from town to town, visiting the believers.

One day while he was with the saints in the town of Lydda, Peter saw a man named Aeneas, who was paralyzed. He had not been out of his bed for eight years.

"Aeneas!" said Peter. "Jesus Christ heals you! Get up and make your bed."

Immediately, Aeneas stood up. Everyone who lived in and near Lydda saw him and turned to the Lord.

Meanwhile in the city of Joppa there was a disciple called Tabitha. She was a woman whose name in Greek was Dorcas. She spent her whole life doing good deeds and helping other people. But one day Dorcas became very sick, and she died. The believers washed her body and laid her in an upstairs room. Then they sent messengers to Lydda, where Peter was visiting.

"Come and see us as soon as you can," they said to Peter.

Peter went back to Joppa with them. When he arrived, they took him to the room where Dorcas was lying. All the widows crowded around him, crying and showing him the shirts and robes she had made while she was alive.

Peter sent them all out of the room, and then he kneeled down and prayed. Then turning to the dead woman, he said, "Tabitha, get up!"

She opened her eyes, saw Peter, and sat up.

Peter took her by the hand and helped her to her feet. Then he called her friends to come and see her.

The news of the miracle spread all over Joppa, and many people believed in the Lord. Peter stayed in Joppa as a guest in the house of a leather tanner named Simon. While he was

there, God did something just as amazing as the
healing of Aeneas and the raising of Dorcas.

In the city of Caesarea lived a Roman officer
named Cornelius. Although he was not a Jew, he
and his whole family and all his servants honored
the Lord God. Cornelius gave many gifts to the
Jewish people, and he prayed all the time.

One day while Cornelius was saying afternoon
prayers in his house, an angel of God suddenly
appeared, dressed in shining clothes. When Cornelius saw the angel standing in front of him, he
was terrified.

"What is it, Lord?" he asked.

"Cornelius," said the angel, "God has heard
your prayers. He has accepted your gifts. Now

you must send to Joppa for a man called Peter. He's staying at the house of Simon the tanner, who lives by the sea."

Then the angel was gone, and Cornelius sent three of his men to Joppa, as the angel had commanded.

The next day, while Cornelius' men were on the way to Joppa, Peter went up to the flat roof of Simon's house to pray. It was about noon, and he began to feel hungry. While lunch was being prepared, Peter saw a vision.

He saw heaven open up and something like a large sheet being lowered to the earth by its four corners. In it were all kinds of animals, reptiles, and birds. All these were creatures that the Jews called unclean. The Jews followed strict rules about eating. They refused to eat with non-Jews, because non-Jews ate unclean foods and didn't follow Jewish laws. They even refused to visit the homes of non-Jews.

Then a voice said to Peter, "Get up, Peter. Kill and eat!"

"Certainly not, Lord!" said Peter. "Never in all my life have I eaten anything unclean."

This happened three times. Then suddenly the sheet was taken back up into heaven.

While Peter was trying to figure out the meaning of this vision, Cornelius' men arrived. They stood at the gate of the house, asking for Peter.

"Listen," the Spirit said to Peter. "Three men are here, looking for you. Get up and go downstairs. Go where they take you, for I myself have sent them."

Peter obeyed the Spirit and went downstairs.

"I'm the man you're looking for," he said to the three strangers. "Why have you come here?"

"Officer Cornelius sent us," they answered. "He's a good man who honors God. All the Jewish people respect him. He was commanded by a holy angel to send for you to come to his house, so he could listen to your message."

Peter invited them to come in and spend the night. The next day he went back with them to Caesarea. Six disciples from Joppa went with him.

When they arrived at Cornelius' house, they found him waiting for them, along with some friends and relatives he had invited to meet Peter. As Peter came into the house, Cornelius went out to meet him. He fell down before Peter and worshiped him.

"Stand up!" said Peter, helping Cornelius to his feet. "I'm only a man."

Then they went into the house, talking together, and Peter met the people who were waiting for him.

He said to them, "You know, according to our religion, a Jew isn't allowed to mix with or even visit people of other nations. But God just showed me in a vision that I must not call anyone unclean. That's why I came as soon as you asked. Now tell me why you have sent for me."

Cornelius told Peter about the angel that had told him to send for Peter. "I did as the angel commanded," he said. "And you have been kind enough to come. Now we're all here in God's presence, and we're ready to hear what the Lord has told you to say."

"Now I see the truth!" said Peter. "God doesn't have favorites. He accepts people in every nation who honor him and do what's right. God sent his message to us, the people of Israel, and he gave us the good news of peace through Jesus Christ, who is Lord of us all.

"Surely you've heard about Jesus," he said. "You must have heard by now what has been going on in Judea. God anointed Jesus with the Holy Spirit and with power. Jesus went around doing good and healing everyone who was in the power of the devil. We are witnesses to everything he did in Judea and Jerusalem.

"They killed Jesus," explained Peter, "but God raised him to life and let him be seen—not by everyone, but by the witnesses God chose. We are those witnesses, we who ate and drank with Jesus after he rose from the dead. Jesus commanded us to preach this good news to the people of Israel, to tell them that Jesus is the one that God has made the judge of the living and the dead. Everyone who believes in him will have their sins forgiven through the power of his name."

While Peter was speaking to them about Jesus,

the Holy Spirit came down on everyone who was listening.

The six Jewish believers who had come with Peter from Joppa were amazed. The gift of the Holy Spirit was being poured out on non-Jews! They could hear the Gentiles speaking in foreign languages and glorifying God!

"Can anyone refuse water baptism to these people?" asked Peter. "They've received the Holy Spirit just the same as we did."

The Gentiles were baptized in the name of Jesus Christ, and Peter stayed with them for a few days.

When Peter returned to Jerusalem, the apostles and other believers asked him what was going on. Some of them criticized him for not making the Gentiles become Jews before they joined the church.

"So!" they said. "You actually visited Gentiles! You even ate with them."

Peter told them all about his vision and the angel that had visited Cornelius. He told them how the Lord had sent him to speak to Cornelius.

"While I was telling them God's message," he said, "the Holy Spirit fell on them—the same as on us. Then I remembered what the Lord Jesus had said: 'John baptized with water, but you will be baptized with the Holy Spirit.' I realized God was giving these Gentiles exactly the same gift that he gave us when we believed in the Lord Jesus Christ. So who was I to try to stop God?"

When they heard this, they stopped criticizing Peter. Instead, they praised God and said, "It is clear that God has given the Gentiles the same chance as he has given us—the chance to turn to him and live!"

What Happened to a Wicked King

Acts 12

HEROD Agrippa was a wicked king like his grandfather, King Herod the Great, and his uncle, King Herod Antipas. Herod the Great had tried to kill Jesus when he was a baby, and Herod Antipas had put John the Baptist to death.

Now Herod Agrippa began to persecute some of the believers. He had James, the brother of the apostle John, put to death by the sword. When he saw that this pleased the Jewish religious leaders, he arrested Peter and put him in jail.

Herod had sixteen soldiers guard Peter. He

was planning to keep Peter in jail until after Passover, and then bring him out for trial.

But the church prayed to God for Peter all the time he was in jail. This is what happened.

The night before Herod was going to bring him to trial, Peter was asleep between two soldiers. He was fastened to them by chains. More soldiers guarded the gates of the prison.

Suddenly an angel of the Lord appeared, and the jail cell was filled with light. The angel tapped Peter on the side and woke him up.

"Hurry!" said the angel. "Get up!"

Immediately the chains fell from Peter's hands.

"Fasten your belt and put on your sandals," said the angel.

Peter did as he was told.

"Wrap your robe around you and follow me," the angel commanded.

Peter followed the angel out. He didn't know whether these things were really happening or whether he was dreaming. They passed by the first guards, then the second, and then they came to the iron gate that led out to the city.

The gate opened all by itself, and they walked out. As they went down the street, the angel suddenly disappeared.

"Now I'm sure!" Peter said out loud. "The Lord sent his angel to rescue me from Herod's power, and from everything the religious leaders hoped would happen to me."

As soon as he realized what was going on, Peter went to the house of Mary, the mother of a disciple named John Mark. Many believers were meeting at her house for prayer.

Peter knocked on the door, and a servant girl named Rhoda came to answer. When she heard his voice, she was so excited and happy, she forgot to open the door. Instead, she ran back inside and told everyone that Peter was standing outside.

"You're out of your mind!" they said to her.

She insisted he was there.

"It must be his angel," they said.

All this time Peter was standing outside, knocking.

When they finally opened the door, they were amazed to see that it was really Peter.

He motioned with his hand for silence. Then he told them how the Lord had brought him out of prison.

"Now," he said, "go and tell James and the others what has happened." Then he left them and went to another place.

The next morning the prison guards were completely confused. They wondered where Peter could be. Herod ordered them to search for Peter, but they couldn't find him. Then Herod had the guards questioned and ordered them to be put to death as punishment for letting the prisoner get away.

Soon afterward King Herod Agrippa left Judea and went to his capital city of Caesarea. He put on his royal robes and sat on his throne and made a speech.

The people were so impressed, they said, "This isn't a man speaking. This is a god!"

At that moment an angel of the Lord struck Herod because he didn't give honor to God. Herod felt such terrible pain, they had to carry him out. He was eaten away by worms and died.

Meanwhile the word of God kept spreading, and the number of believers grew larger and larger.

More Stories
About Paul

11

The Holy Spirit Sends Paul and Barnabas

Acts 11, 13

WHEN Saul was persecuting the church, the believers scattered to places as far away as Phoenicia, Cyprus, and Antioch. As they fled, they shared the gospel of Jesus Christ with the Jews who lived in those places.

In the city of Antioch, the believers shared the good news with Gentiles as well as with Jews. The power of the Lord was with them, and a large number of people believed and turned to the Lord.

When the church in Jerusalem heard about

this, they sent Barnabas to Antioch to investigate. Barnabas was a good man, filled with the Holy Spirit and faith. When he saw what God was doing in Antioch, he was delighted. He encouraged the new believers to be faithful and true to the Lord. Then he went up to Tarsus to look for Saul.

Barnabas found Saul and brought him back to Antioch. For a whole year Barnabas and Saul worked together, teaching the new believers.

The people who believed in Jesus called themselves, "saints," "brothers and sisters," "disciples," and "followers of the way." The Jews called them "Nazarenes." In Antioch they were called by a new name: "Christians."

One day while the Christians were worshiping the Lord and fasting, the Holy Spirit told them, "Set Barnabas and Saul apart for me to do my work."

They prayed and fasted some more. Then they laid their hands on Barnabas and Saul, to set them apart for God's work. And so these two began the first missionary journey.

They took John Mark with them as their helper and went by ship to the island of Cyprus. At Salamis, the main city, they preached the word of God in the Jewish synagogue.

Then they left Salamis and traveled across the island to the city of Paphos, where the Roman governor lived. There they met a Jewish magician named Bar-Jesus, who was pretending to

be a prophet. He was an intelligent man, a friend of Sergius Paulus, the governor of Cyprus.

Sergius Paulus sent for Barnabas and Saul, for he was eager to hear the word of God. But the magician, whose Greek name was Elymas, tried to stop them. He didn't want Paulus to accept the Christian faith.

Then Saul was filled with the Holy Spirit. He stared at Elymas and said, "You son of the devil! You enemy of true religion! You monster of evil tricks! It's time you stopped trying to twist the truth of the Lord into lies. Now the Lord's hand will strike you, and you'll become blind. For a while you won't be able to see the light of the sun."

Immediately, Elymas felt everything become misty and dark. He reached around, trying to find someone to lead him by the hand. When Sergius Paulus saw this, he was so impressed, he became a believer.

From that time on, Saul stopped using his Hebrew name. Instead, he was known by his Greek name, Paul. Paul became the leader of the mission to the non-Jews, the apostle to the Gentiles.

Light for the Gentiles

Acts 13—14

PAUL and Barnabas and their helper, John Mark, sailed from Cyprus to Asia Minor. When they reached the town of Perga in the province of Pamphylia, John Mark left and went back to Jerusalem.

Paul and Barnabas continued their journey. They followed the Roman roads through the mountain passes and up into the hills of Galatia, to the city of Antioch-Pisidia.

On the Sabbath day they went to the synagogue and sat down. After the lessons were read, the leaders of the synagogue welcomed Paul and Barnabas.

"Brothers," they said, "if you have any words of encouragement for the congregation, please speak to us."

Paul stood, held up his hand for silence, and began to speak. "Men of Israel and all Gentiles who have come here to worship God," he said, "listen to me." He told them how God had chosen Israel to be his people, and how he had sent Jesus to save them. God had kept his promises to Israel by raising Jesus from the dead, said Paul.

"Don't make the same mistake as your ancestors!" he warned. "They refused to believe God's message."

After the service, as Paul and Barnabas were leaving the synagogue, the people kept asking them to come back again the next week and tell them more about Jesus. Paul and Barnabas talked to the many people who followed them out. They encouraged them to trust God.

The next week on the Sabbath day almost everyone in the city came to the synagogue to hear God's message. When the Jews saw the crowds, they were so jealous, they argued with Paul and insulted him.

Paul and Barnabas answered harshly, "We had to speak God's message to you first. But since you don't want it, we'll leave you and go to the Gentiles. After all, that's what the Lord commanded when he said in the Scriptures:

I have made you a light for the Gentiles,
  to take my salvation to the ends of the earth."

The Gentiles were happy to hear Paul, and they thanked the Lord for the message. Many became believers, and the Lord's message spread all over the countryside.

But the Jews stirred up the leading men and the upper-class women who worshiped God. They forced Paul and Barnabas to move on.

Paul and Barnabas just shook the dust from their feet as they left Antioch-Pisidia and headed for the next city. The disciples they left behind were filled with joy and the Holy Spirit.

The next city was Iconium, where Paul and Barnabas stayed for a long time. Many Jews and Gentiles who heard them speak in the synagogue became believers, and many people listened to their message.

But then the unbelieving Jews stirred up the people and turned them against Paul and Barnabas and the believers. Paul and Barnabas kept on speaking boldly for the Lord, and the Lord showed that he was with them by giving them the power to work miracles.

The people of the city were divided. Some agreed with the unbelieving Jews, and some with the apostles. A group of Gentiles and Jews joined with the leaders of the city and agreed to insult Paul and Barnabas and stone them. When Paul and Barnabas heard about their plot, they left

Iconium and went to the city of Lystra.

In Lystra they saw a man who had never walked. His feet were crippled by a birth defect. The man sat and listened to Paul's preaching, and Paul looked into his face. He saw that the man had the faith to be healed.

"Stand up straight on your feet!" Paul said.

The man jumped up and started to walk around.

When the crowd saw what Paul had done, they shouted, "The gods have come down to us in human form!"

They began to call Barnabas Zeus, the king of the gods, and they called Paul Hermes, the messenger of the gods.

Someone went to the temple of Zeus and brought back the priests, who came with oxen ready to be sacrificed. The people wanted to offer the oxen as sacrifice to the "gods" Paul and Barnabas.

When Paul and Barnabas realized what was happening, they were horrified. They tore their clothes and ran into the middle of the crowd.

"Friends!" they said. "Why are you doing this? We're only human, just like you! We came here to tell the good news about the kingdom of God. We want you to turn away from these worthless gods of yours and worship the living God—the God who made heaven and earth and the sea, and everything in them.

"In the past, God let every nation go its own way and worship whatever they wanted. But he gave proof of himself by the good things he does. He gives rain from heaven, and he makes your crops grow in the right seasons. He gives you food, and he fills you with happiness."

But even with this speech of Paul's, the apostles just barely managed to stop the people from offering sacrifices to them.

Some time later some unbelieving Jews from Antioch-Pisidia and Iconium came to Lystra and turned the people against Paul and Barnabas. They stoned Paul and dragged him out of the city. They thought he was dead.

The believers gathered in a circle around Paul, and he stood up and walked back to town.

The next day Paul and Barnabas went to Derbe. There they preached the gospel and made many disciples. Then they went back the way they had come.

They traveled through the cities of Galatia, strengthening the believers and encouraging them to remain true to the faith. They told the believers about the difficult times that would come. The Gentile Christians will suffer in the future as the Jewish Christians have already, they warned.

"It is only through many troubles that we enter the kingdom of God," they said.

Paul and Barnabas chose people in each church to be leaders. Then they prayed and fasted and asked the Lord to watch over them.

They preached God's message in Perga, and then they sailed back to Syria. They reached Antioch a year and a half after they had left.

They gathered the church together and told them about their adventures in Cyprus and Galatia. They told how God was opening the door of faith to the Gentiles.

13

The Apostles' Meeting in Jerusalem

Acts 15; Galatians

YOU can't be saved unless you become a Jew!"

"No, that's not necessary! God accepts Gentiles who believe in Jesus Christ. Gentiles don't have to become Jews first!"

Paul and Barnabas were arguing with some Jewish Christians who had come to Antioch from Judea. These people were upsetting the Gentile Christians by saying they had to become Jews.

How could they settle this argument? Who would decide?

God told Paul to go to Jerusalem and ask the leaders of the church there for help. The Christians in Antioch agreed to send Barnabas and some others with Paul, and they set off. As they traveled through Phoenicia and Samaria, they cheered the believers by telling them how the Gentiles were turning to God. Then they arrived in Jerusalem.

After they were welcomed by the church and the apostles, they told them what God had been doing through them, and how the Gentiles were becoming believers.

Some Pharisees who were believers didn't like what Paul and Barnabas were doing. These people were members of a strict group of teachers of the Jewish law. They were sure that God wanted the Gentiles to be just like them, to follow all the rules and customs of the Jewish people first, and then become believers in Jesus Christ.

"The Gentiles must become Jews!" they said. "They must obey the law of Moses as carefully as we do."

The apostles and elders of the Jerusalem church met and talked about the problem. After a long discussion, Peter stood up and spoke to them.

"My brothers," he said, "you know that God chose me from the earliest days to tell his message to the Gentiles so they would become believers. Remember how officer Cornelius became

a believer. God showed us plainly that he wants the Gentiles to believe. He gave them the Holy Spirit, just as he gave us. He made no difference between them and us.

"So why are you annoying God by making these Gentiles carry the burden of the law? You know perfectly well that our ancestors had trouble obeying the law, and so did we. It's a burden we couldn't carry. Here's what's important: we're saved by faith, through Jesus Christ, just the same as the Gentiles."

After Peter spoke, everyone was silent as they thought about what he had said.

Then Barnabas and Paul told them about the miracles God had worked among the Gentiles.

Everyone listened carefully, and then the meeting was quiet again.

Then James said, "Listen to me, brothers! What Peter says is the same as what God says in the Scriptures. Let's not make it any harder for the Gentile. Let's just ask them to follow a few rules, so they can eat with Jewish Christians."

Everyone agreed not to make the Gentile believers follow the Jewish law. James and Peter and John, the "pillars of the church" in Jerusalem, shook hands with Paul and Barnabas. They all agreed that Paul and Barnabas should preach to the Gentiles and the others should take the gospel to the Jews.

The leaders of the Jerusalem church sent Judas Barsabbas and Silas back to Antioch with Paul and Barnabas. When they arrived, they told the community about the apostles' meeting in Jerusalem. The Gentiles were glad to hear that they didn't have to follow the Jewish law. Judas and Silas encouraged and strengthened the believers in Antioch, and then they returned to Jerusalem.

A while later Peter came up to Antioch. At first he ate with Gentile believers, but when some of James' friends came, he stopped, and so did Barnabas. Paul was so annoyed, he scolded Peter in front of the others.

"Although you're a Jew, you live like a Gentile," he said. "So why are you trying to make the Gentiles live like Jews?"

It was a hard problem. The leaders of the church agreed that God didn't have favorites, that he gave the Holy Spirit to Gentiles as well as Jews. But it took a long time for this idea to be accepted. The strict Jewish believers wanted to be good Jews, and they wanted the Gentiles to follow the same rules.

Paul wrote a letter to the Gentile Christians in Galatia. He warned them not to listen to people who told them to follow the Jewish law. The important thing is not following rules, said Paul. The important thing is living by faith in Jesus.

Paul encouraged the Galatians to live their whole lives in the power of the Holy Spirit. The Spirit gives freedom, he said. The Spirit produces fruit in people's lives. These fruits are
love,
joy,
peace,
patience,
kindness,
goodness,
faithfulness,
humility,
and self-control.

14

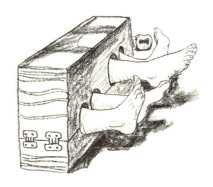

"Come Over to Macedonia!"

Acts 15—16

PAUL was thinking about the believers in Galatia. He was wondering how they were, and he wanted to see them again.

"Let's go back," he said to Barnabas. "Let's visit the believers in the cities where we preached, to see how they're doing."

Barnabas agreed to go, and he wanted to take John Mark with them. But Paul refused to travel with John Mark because he had left them before the end of their first missionary journey.

The three men disagreed so much, they separated. Barnabas took John Mark to Cyprus, and Paul took Silas on his second missionary journey.

After the Antioch church gave Paul and Silas their blessing, they traveled through Syria and Cilicia. They strengthened the believers in those provinces, and then they went to Derbe and Lystra.

At the town of Lystra a young disciple named Timothy joined them. His mother, Eunice, and his grandmother, Lois, were Jewish Christians, and his father was a Greek. The Christians of Lystra and Iconium had great respect for Timothy. He became Paul's friend and helper for the rest of Paul's life. They were as close as a father and son.

Paul and Silas and Timothy traveled through all the cities where Paul and Barnabas had preached. They told the believers about the meeting in Jerusalem, and how it had been decided that Gentile Christians didn't have to become Jews. Because of their visit, the churches grew stronger in the faith, and more people joined them every day.

The three missionaries went on through Phrygia and Galatia, ready to preach to the Gentiles in any place the Holy Spirit led them. But when the Holy Spirit stopped them from preaching in the provinces of Asia, Mysia, and Bithynia, Paul didn't know what to do. He knew the Spirit of Jesus was telling them not to preach in those places, but where should they go?

When they reached the city of Troas, Paul had a vision. He saw a man from Macedonia, standing and begging him, "Come over to Macedonia and help us!"

Now Paul and his friends knew what God wanted them to do: they must preach the gospel in Macedonia. So they sailed across the Aegean Sea from Troas to Macedonia. They took their friend Luke with them. He was a doctor and a traveling companion of Paul for many years.

Their ship stopped at the island of Samothrace, where they spent the night. Then they sailed on to Neapolis, where they left the ship and traveled by land to the city of Philippi.

The four friends stayed in Philippi a few days. On the Sabbath they wanted to worship. Since there was no synagogue in that town, they went down to the riverside, where they expected to find a place for prayer. They sat down and talked to the women who were meeting there.

One of their listeners was a woman named Lydia. She was a merchant who bought and sold purple cloth. She already worshiped God, and now the Lord opened her heart to accept Paul's message.

After Lydia and her family and servants were baptized, she said, "If you think I'm a true believer, come down to my house and stay with us." They accepted her invitation.

One day while Paul and his friends were going to the place of prayer, they met a slave girl who

had an evil spirit. The spirit gave her the power
to know the future, and she earned a lot of money
for her owners by telling fortunes.

The girl started to follow Paul and his friends.
She shouted, "These men are servants of the
highest God! They have come to tell you how to
be saved!"

She did this every day until finally Paul was so
annoyed, he turned around and said to the spirit
in her, "In the name of Jesus Christ, I command
you to come out of her!" It came out immediately.

But when the girl's owners realized that they
wouldn't be able to make any more money from
her fortune-telling, they were furious. They
grabbed Paul and Silas and took them to the

Roman officials in the marketplace.

"These men are Jews," they said. "They're causing a lot of trouble in our city. They're teaching things that are against the law for us Roman citizens."

The crowd in the marketplace joined in the attack on Paul and Silas. The officials had the two of them stripped of their clothes and beaten with wooden rods. After they were beaten hard, they were thrown into jail. The officials told the jailer to watch them carefully. The jailer locked them in the dungeon and fastened their feet between heavy blocks of wood.

About midnight Paul and Silas were praying and singing songs of praise to God, and the other prisoners were listening to them. Suddenly there was a great earthquake, strong enough to shake the foundations of the prison. Immediately all the doors flew open, and the chains fell off all the prisoners.

The jailer woke up, and when he saw the doors open, he pulled out his sword. He was going to kill himself, because he thought the prisoners had escaped and he would be blamed.

But Paul called out to him in a loud voice, "Don't hurt yourself! We're all here!"

The jailer ordered some lights and rushed in, trembling all over. He fell at the feet of Paul and Silas, and then he led them out of the dungeon.

"Sirs," he said, "what must I do to be saved?"

"Believe in the Lord Jesus," they answered.

"Then you will be saved. You and all your family and servants."

They preached God's message to the jailer and all his family and servants. Right then and there, in the jail in the middle of the night, he took them and washed their wounds, and he and all his family were baptized. Then he took them into his own house and gave them food. He and his whole household were overjoyed at finding faith in God.

When morning came, the Roman officials sent their police to the jail with orders to let Paul and Silas go. The jailer said to Paul, "The officials have sent a message that you can be set free. Now you can leave this place and go on your way in peace."

But Paul refused to leave that way. Instead, he said to the police, "They beat us publicly without giving us any kind of a trial. They threw us into prison even though we're Roman citizens. And now they want us to leave quietly! Well, they can't get rid of us that easily. They'll have to come take us out themselves."

When the police took Paul's message back to the officials, and the officials were frightened to hear that Paul and Silas were Roman citizens. They came in person to the jail and apologized and let them out. Then they politely asked them to leave the city.

Paul and Silas left Philippi, but first they went to Lydia's house, where they met with the believers and gave them encouragement.

15

Turning the World Upside Down

Acts 17—18; 1 Corinthians 1—3, 16; 1 and 2 Thessalonians

PAUL and his friends traveled across Macedonia from Philippi to the city of Thessalonica. In this great city they found many Jews, and they visited the synagogue on the Sabbath.

For three Sabbaths in a row Paul argued with the Jews from the Scriptures. He showed them why it was necessary for the Messiah to die and rise again from the dead. Then he said, "This Jesus whom I am telling you about is the Messiah!"

Some of the Jews became believers, and so did

many Gentile men and upper-class women. Paul settled down in the city to build the church. He worked at his trade of tentmaking to support himself, and several times the believers in Philippi helped him by sending him money.

But then some of the unbelieving Jews became jealous. They were so angry, they decided to get rid of Paul. They gathered some loafers from the city streets and stirred up a mob until the whole city was upset. They led the mob to the house of a man named Jason, where they expected to find Paul and Silas. When they couldn't find them, they forced Jason and some of the believers to go with them to the city officials.

As they dragged the believers to the officials, they shouted, "These are the men who have turned the world upside down! Now they've come here, and Jason has taken them into his house. What's worse, they've broken the laws of the emperor! They say there's another king, a king named Jesus!"

The people and the rulers of Thessalonica were upset when they heard these things. They made Jason and the other believers pay a fine, and then they let them go. But it was too dangerous for Paul and Silas to stay in Thessalonica. So that night, as soon as it was dark, the believers sent them to Berea.

When they reached Berea they went to the synagogue. They found the Jews of Berea open-minded and ready to listen eagerly to Paul's message. Every day they studied the Scriptures to see whether what Paul was saying was true. Many of them became believers, along with a large number of upper-class Greek women and some Greek men.

But when the Jews of Thessalonica found out that Paul was preaching in Berea, they came after him. Timothy came, too, and warned Paul that he should leave the city.

While Silas and Timothy stayed in Berea, the believers took Paul to Athens, in the province of Achaia. Then they returned to Berea with a message for Silas and Timothy to join Paul as soon as possible.

While Paul waited in Athens for Silas and Timothy, he walked around the city. He saw the famous Greek temples and statues, including the statue of the goddess Athena in the temple of the Parthenon.

Paul was so disgusted by the sight of all these idols, he felt he had to talk to the people in the synagogue. He also argued in the open market-place with the passersby. While he was speaking, some Greek philosophers came and made fun of him.

"What's this idiot babbling about?" some of them asked.

Others answered, "He seems to be talking about some new gods—some really strange ones!"

Paul was actually preaching about Jesus and

his resurrection, but the Greeks thought "resurrection" was the name of a goddess.

But they were curious, so they took Paul to a hill nearby, where the city council met. There the town leaders asked him, "Would you tell us what this new teaching of yours is all about? It sounds strange to us, and we want to know what it means."

The Athenians loved anything that was new and different. They spent all their time gossiping about the latest thing.

"Gentlemen of Athens!" said Paul as he stood in the middle of their council. "I have seen with my own eyes that in every way you are very religious. As I walked around your city and looked at the objects you worship, I noticed that you have an altar on which it is written: 'To the Unknown God.' This God you worship without knowing is the God I am here to tell you about! This God made the world and everything in it. He is ruler of heaven and earth. He doesn't live in temples made by human hands. He doesn't need anything made by human beings. He doesn't need anything at all, for he is the one who gives everything, including our life and breath.

"This God created all races from one ancestor. He controls their history, for he wants them to look for him and find him. And all the time, he isn't far away.

"In the past God has overlooked your idol-making. But now he commands all people everywhere

to turn from their idols and worship him. For he has set a day when the whole world will be judged by a man he has chosen. He has proved this by raising that man from the dead!"

When the Athenians heard Paul speak about someone being raised from the dead, they began to laugh out loud.

But some of them said, "We want to hear more about this."

Paul left the city council meeting, and some of the Athenians went with him and accepted the Christian faith. Among these were Dionysius, a member of the council, and a woman named Damaris.

Paul didn't stay long in Athens. He went south

to the great city of Corinth, a busy trading center. There he met Aquila and Priscilla. They were a Jewish couple who had just arrived from Italy. They had left Rome because Emperor Claudius had ordered all the Jews to leave.

When Paul visited Aquila and Priscilla in their house, he learned that they were tentmakers, as he was. He stayed with them, and together they earned their living by sewing tent cloth from tough black goathair.

Every Sabbath day Paul spoke in the synagogue at Corinth, trying to convince people to believe in Jesus. By the time Silas and Timothy finally arrived from Macedonia, Paul was spending all his time preaching.

Then the Jews of Corinth turned against Paul and insulted him. Paul answered them by taking his cloak and shaking it out in front of them.

"You're to blame if you die!" he said. "From now on I'm going to the Gentiles with a perfectly clear conscience!"

He left them and went to the house of a believer named Titus Justus, who lived next door to the synagogue. Crispus, the leader of the synagogue, became a believer, along with his whole family and many other Corinthians.

One night in Corinth the Lord spoke to Paul in a vision. "Don't be afraid," he said. "Keep on speaking. Don't let anyone silence you, for I am with you. No one will be able to hurt you. There are many people in this city who belong to me."

After this some people did try to silence Paul. They had him arrested and taken to the Roman governor. But they weren't able to hurt him. Gallio, the governor, refused to pay attention to their charges against Paul.

Paul stayed in Corinth for a year and a half. He taught God's message and built the church. While he was there, he wrote two letters to the Christians in Thessalonica. He praised them for their good example. They were putting away their idols and telling other people the good news about Jesus.

Paul decided to visit Syria. He took Priscilla and Aquila with him. When their ship stopped at Ephesus, Paul went to the synagogue and debated with the Jews. They asked him to stay longer, but he refused. Then he said, "If it is God's will, I'll be back another time."

He left Priscilla and Aquila in Ephesus and went on his way. He visited Jerusalem and Antioch, and then, a few months later, he left on his third missionary journey. He made his way through Galatia and Phrygia, visiting the churches, and headed back for Ephesus.

16

Good News for Asia

Acts 18—19

A JEWISH believer named Apollos came to Ephesus. He spoke powerfully to the people and taught them about Jesus Christ. Apollos was an educated man who knew the Scriptures well. He had learned the way of the Lord Jesus, but he knew only the baptism of John, with water.

Paul's friends Priscilla and Aquila heard Apollos speaking boldly about Jesus in the synagogue, and they took him aside and explained to him more about the way of God.

After that Apollos went to the province of Achaia. He took along a letter from the believers of Ephesus to the believers of Corinth, to introduce him. When he arrived at Corinth, he helped the believers there and strengthened them in their faith. With his strong arguments, he defeated the nonbelieving Jews in debates, because he could show them from the Scriptures that Jesus was the Messiah.

While Apollos was at Corinth, Paul arrived back at Ephesus. He found twelve new disciples, people who had been taught by Apollos.

He asked them, "Did you receive the Holy Spirit when you became believers?"

"No," they answered. "We have never even heard of the Holy Spirit."

"Well, then," said Paul, "how were you baptized?"

"With John's baptism," they answered. "With water."

"John's baptism was for repentance," said Paul. "It was a sign that you turned away from your sins. But John said that we must believe in the one who came after him—in Jesus."

When they heard this, the disciples were baptized in the name of the Lord Jesus. Paul laid his hands on them, and the Holy Spirit came on them, and they began to speak in foreign languages and prophesy.

Paul stayed in Ephesus, speaking boldly in the synagogue. For three months he argued with the people, and many of them were convinced. But then some of them hardened their hearts. They refused to believe the message, and they publicly insulted the way of the Lord.

Paul left the synagogue. He took his followers to another building, and there he held discussions and taught for two years. Many people heard God's message while Paul was teaching in Ephesus.

Meanwhile, other missionaries were preaching in the nearby cities of Colossai, Laodicea, and Hieropolis. Soon everyone in the whole province of Asia had heard the word of the Lord.

God worked miracles through Paul whi'e he was in Ephesus. The Ephesians were so impressed, they took handkerchiefs and clothing that he had touched and gave them to people who were sick and people who had evil spirits, and they were healed.

But there were many magicians in Ephesus. Some Jews who traveled from town to town, working magic, came to Ephesus. They tried to drive out evil spirits by trying to call on the name of the Lord Jesus. They said to the evil spirits, "We command you in the name of Jesus, whom Paul preaches." These men were seven sons of a priest named Sceva.

Then one time the evil spirit answered, "I know Jesus, and I've heard of Paul, but who are you?"

The man who had the evil spirit attacked the magicians so violently that he overpowered all seven of them. They rushed out of the house,

wounded and with their clothes torn off their backs.

When the people of Ephesus heard about this, a feeling of holy fear came over them, and the name of the Lord Jesus was greatly respected.

Many of the believers began to admit that they had been practicing magic. They collected their books about magic and burned them in public. The value of these books was more than fifty thousand pieces of silver. In this way the word of the Lord kept spreading and growing stronger.

Trouble in Corinth and a Riot in Ephesus

Acts 19—20; 1 and 2 Corinthians; Colossians 4

WHILE Paul was living in Ephesus, he was concerned about the believers in Corinth. The church in Corinth was growing fast, but the believers were having serious problems. Many people were copying the wicked behavior of the pagans around them. Others were misusing the spiritual gifts that God had given.

So Paul wrote a letter to help the Corinthians. He reminded them that God gives gifts to build up the whole church, not just certain people. He told them that love is the most important of all the spiritual gifts, even more important than knowledge.

"In this life," wrote Paul, "we have three things that last: faith, hope, and love. And the greatest of these is love."

Paul was planning to stay in Ephesus until late spring. Then suddenly his work was interrupted by a great riot.

A silversmith named Demetrius had a successful business making models of the temple of Artemis, the great mother goddess of Asia Minor. This business earned large profits for Demetrius and his workers. But when the people of Ephesus began to believe in Jesus, they stopped worshiping Artemis. They stopped buying Demetrius' silver models.

Finally Demetrius called together his workers, along with some other people in the same business. "Men," he said, "you all know how our business success depends on this work. If you've been paying attention, you've noticed what this man Paul has been doing. Why, he's been convincing people all over the province of Asia that gods made by human hands aren't real gods. This is hurting our business! It's also hurting the temple of the great goddess Artemis. That's not all—something even worse could happen! The greatness of the goddess Artemis could be destroyed—the goddess who is worshiped by everyone in Asia, by everyone in the world!"

When the workers heard Demetrius' speech,

they were furious. They began to shout, "Great is Artemis of the Ephesians!"

Soon the whole city was rioting. A mob gathered and rushed to the great outdoor theater in the middle of the city. They grabbed two of Paul's friends and dragged them into the theater. Paul wanted to go into the crowd, but the believers wouldn't let him. Some of Paul's friends who were important officials begged him not to go to the theater.

At the theater, some people were shouting one thing and some were shouting another. The whole meeting was confused. Most of the mob had no idea why they were there.

A Jew named Alexander tried to speak to the

crowd, but when they realized he was a Jew, they drowned him out by shouting, "Great is Artemis of the Ephesians!" They kept this up for two hours.

Finally the town clerk calmed down the crowd. "Men of Ephesus!" he said. "Everyone knows that our city is the center of the worship of the great Artemis, and the guardian of her temple. No one can deny it. Now, don't do anything you'll be sorry for later. These Christians aren't doing anything to the temple. They haven't insulted our goddess. So why have you brought them here? If Demetrius and the silversmiths want to bring charges, let them do it in court. If you citizens have any complaints, take them to the regular town meeting. Right now we're all in danger of being charged with rioting! There's no excuse for this!"

When the town clerk was finished with his speech, he sent the people home.

After the riot, Paul changed his travel plans. Instead of waiting until late spring, he decided to leave right away for a visit to Macedonia, Achaia, Jerusalem, and Rome. He called the believers together, encouraged them, and said good-bye.

Paul traveled through Macedonia and Achaia, collecting money for the poor people in the Jerusalem church. When he reached Corinth and saw how the believers were behaving, he felt discouraged. He went back to Macedonia and wrote a second letter to the Corinthians.

In his letter Paul scolded the Corinthians. He told them he cared about them, but he was terribly upset about their behavior and wanted them to remain faithful.

In the same letter Paul told them about a problem he had, which he called his "thorn in the flesh." He had begged the Lord three times to remove it, but the Lord had told him, "My grace is enough for you." Paul didn't explain exactly what his problem was.

Paul sent the letter to Corinth with his friend Titus. When Titus returned to Macedonia, he reported that the Corinthians were stronger in the faith and Paul felt much better.

18

Paul's Journey to Jerusalem

Acts 20—21; Romans

PAUL returned to Corinth to teach the believers and collect money to take to the poor in the church at Jerusalem. From Corinth he wrote a long letter to the church in Rome.

In his letter to the Romans, Paul wrote about living by faith. Both Jews and Gentiles need faith, he said. Paul loved the Jewish people very much and he wrote about his hopes for them. In God's family, said Paul, the Jews were like the older son, and the Gentiles were like the younger child. Paul asked the Roman believers to send money to the poor Jewish believers in Jerusalem. The Gentiles owed much to the Jews, he said, because the Jewish believers had brought them the good news about Jesus.

Paul was planning to take the collection of money from all the churches to Jerusalem. After that he hoped to go to Spain. In those days Spain was at the edge of the civilized world. It was considered to be "the ends of the earth."

While Paul was staying in Corinth, some unbelieving Jews began to plot against him. He decided to change his travel plans. Instead of going directly to Jerusalem, he returned to Macedonia and then headed for the coast of Asia Minor. His friends Timothy and Luke were traveling with him, and so were men from the Gentile churches who were helping take the money to Jerusalem.

When he reached the city of Troas, Paul met with the believers at their usual evening meeting on the first day of the week. They broke bread together, and then Paul began to speak to them. Since he was going to leave the next morning, he kept on talking. It got dark, it was almost midnight, and he was still talking. Many lamps were burning in the upstairs room where they were meeting.

A young man named Eutychus was sitting in the window. As Paul talked on and on, Eutychus became sleepier and sleepier. Finally he fell sound asleep. He fell out of the window to the ground, three stories below. When they picked him up, he was dead.

Paul went down and bent over him and held him gently in his arms. "Don't worry," he said. "There's still life in him!"

Then Paul went back upstairs, had something to eat, and went on talking. Finally the sun came up and Paul left. The boy Eutychus was taken home alive, and everyone was relieved.

Paul and his friends traveled by ship down the coast of Asia Minor, stopping at Chios, Samos, and Trogyllium. They were in a hurry to reach Jerusalem in time for the feast of Pentecost, so they didn't stop at Ephesus. But when they reached the town of Miletus, Paul sent a message to the leaders of the Ephesian church. He asked them to come and meet with him, for he wanted to talk to them one more time and tell them good-bye.

When the Ephesians arrived, Paul told them that he was going to Jerusalem because the Holy Spirit was telling him to go. He didn't know what would happen there, but the Holy Spirit had warned him that jail and persecution were waiting for him in every city. He didn't care about his own life. He just wanted to finish the mission the Lord Jesus had given him—the mission to preach the gospel.

Then Paul gave the Ephesians some advice and warnings. Finally he said, "I turn you over to the Lord's care, and to the message of his grace. That message can build you up and give you your place among the saints of God."

When Paul finished speaking, he kneeled down with his friends and prayed. They were all crying as they hugged him and kissed him good-bye. They were especially sad because he said they would never see him again.

Then Paul and his friends sailed on their way. They made short stops at the islands of Cos and Rhodes, and then they changed ships at Patara. They went on board a large cargo ship that was sailing to Phoenicia.

They sailed past Cyprus on to the port of Tyre, where their ship spent a week. While the sailors unloaded the ship's cargo, Paul and his friends visited the believers in Tyre. Those believers warned Paul not to go to Jerusalem. But at the end of the week Paul and his friends went on their way.

The believers and their families went with them all the way out of the city. When they reached the beach, they kneeled down to pray. Then they said good-bye. The believers went back to Tyre and Paul and his friends went on board the ship.

From Tyre they sailed to Ptolemais, where they stayed overnight with some believers. The next morning they traveled by land to Caesarea. There they stayed at the house of Philip the evangelist. Philip had four unmarried daughters who were prophets.

After they had been at Philip's house a few days, a prophet named Agabus came from Judea to see them. He took Paul's belt and tied his own hands and feet with it.

"The Holy Spirit says this!" said Agabus. "The owner of this belt will be tied by the Jews in Jerusalem, and they will hand him over to the Gentiles."

When Paul's friends and the believers in Caesarea heard this prophecy, they begged him not to go to Jerusalem.

"Don't upset me with your tears!" he said. "I'm ready to be tied up, and even to die, for the sake of the Lord Jesus!"

Since they couldn't change his mind, they just said, "May the Lord's will be done."

106

19

Paul Is Arrested

Acts 21—23

THE believers in Jerusalem welcomed Paul and his friends and invited them to stay with them. Paul visited James and the other leaders and told them about all the wonderful things God was doing among the Gentiles.

When they heard Paul's report, they glorified God. Then they warned Paul, "Brother, many Jews have become believers, and all of them are loyal to the law of Moses. They've been told that you teach Jews who live in Gentile lands to ignore Jewish law and customs. They'll find out

107

that you're here in Jerusalem, and then who knows what might happen?

"You should follow our advice and stay out of trouble. Do something to show these people that you're a good Jew. Here are four men who have taken a vow. Go with them to the temple and pay the cost of their vow-finishing ceremony. That will stop the wicked rumors that you don't obey the Jewish law."

The next day Paul went to the temple and paid for the four men's sacrifices. He made arrangements to return to the temple in seven days, when the sacrifices would be offered. (This was usual when someone made a vow to God.)

That week the unbelieving Jews heard that Paul was in Jerusalem with some Gentile believers and the money they had collected from the Gentile churches. Some of Paul's old enemies, unbelieving Jews from Asia, were in Jerusalem, and they saw a chance to get rid of Paul. They decided to accuse him of the crime of taking a Gentile into the forbidden places of the temple.

It was against the law for a Gentile to enter the inner courtyards of the temple, or the temple building itself. There were signs in Latin, Greek, and Hebrew warning foreigners that if they entered the Jewish part of the temple area, they would be put to death.

After a week, Paul returned to the temple. The Jews from Asia were waiting for him. They stirred up the crowd and grabbed Paul.

"Men of Israel!" they shouted. "Help! This is the man who is going everywhere preaching against our people, our law, and our temple. Now he has brought Gentiles into the temple. He has made our holy place unclean!"

The whole city was upset. A mob came running and grabbed Paul. They dragged him out of the temple and slammed the gates behind him. While they were trying to kill Paul, the commander of the nearby Roman fortress heard the riot. He called out his soldiers and sent them running down the steps from the fortress to the temple.

When the mob saw the Roman soldiers, they stopped beating Paul. The Roman commander, Claudius Lysias, went up to Paul and arrested him. He ordered his men to tie Paul with two chains.

"Who is this man, and what has he done?" Lysias asked the mob.

Some of them shouted one thing, and some of them shouted another. There was so much noise, Lysias couldn't tell what was going on. He ordered his men to take Paul up to the fortress. By the time they reached the top of the steps, the mob was so violent, the soldiers had to lift Paul up and carry him away.

"Kill him!" the people shouted as they rushed after Paul.

Just as the soldiers were taking Paul into the fortress, he asked Lysias, "May I say something?"

Lysias answered, "So you speak Greek! I thought you were that Egyptian who started the revolt recently and led those four thousand terrorists into the desert."

"I'm a Jew," answered Paul. "I'm a citizen of Tarsus, an important city in Cilicia. Please give me permission to speak to the people."

Lysias gave Paul permission, and Paul stood at the top of the steps and motioned for the crowd to be quiet. Then he spoke to them in the Hebrew language.

"My brothers and fathers," he said. "Listen to what I have to say to defend myself."

As soon as they heard him speaking to them in their own language, they became very still.

"I'm a Jew," said Paul. "I was born in Tarsus in Cilicia, but I grew up here in this city." He told them how he was a strict Pharisee, and how he had persecuted the church. He told them that Jesus had spoken to him and sent him to preach the gospel to the Gentiles.

As soon as Paul said that the Lord had sent him to the Gentiles, the people began to shout, "Kill him! Rid the earth of such a man! He isn't fit to live!"

They were screaming and ripping their clothes and throwing dust into the air to show that they rejected him.

Lysias ordered his men to take Paul into the fortress and whip him, to make him confess. When they tied him up to be whipped, Paul spoke

to the officer in charge.

"Is it legal for you to whip a man who is a Roman citizen?" he asked. "Especially one who hasn't even had a trial?"

When the officer heard this, he went to Lysias and said, "Do you know what you were about to do? That man is a Roman citizen!"

(In the Roman Empire, some people had the privileges of citizenship, with rights to trial and lesser punishments for crimes.)

Commander Lysias went to Paul. "Tell me," he asked. "Are you a Roman citizen?"

"I am," answered Paul.

"It cost me a lot of money to buy my citizenship," said Lysias.

"I was born a Roman citizen," said Paul.

Then the men who were going to question Paul left in a hurry. Even Lysias was upset to discover that he had put a Roman citizen in chains.

The next day Lysias ordered the Jewish council to meet and hear Paul, so he could find out what was going on.

Paul looked at the council and said, "My brothers, I have lived my life so far with a clear conscience before God."

Then Ananias the high priest ordered the men standing near Paul to hit him on the mouth.

"God will punish you, you whitewashed wall!" said Paul. "How dare you sit there judging me by the law, while you break the law by ordering them to hit me!"

They answered, "You're insulting God's high priest!"

"Brothers," answered Paul, "I didn't know he was the high priest. Of course, Scripture tells us not to speak against our rulers."

Then Paul noticed that some of the members of the Jewish ruling council were Sadducees, and some of them were Pharisees.

"Brothers," he said to them, "I'm a Pharisee and the son of Pharisees. I'm on trial here because I believe what the Pharisees teach: I believe in the resurrection of the dead."

As soon as he said this, the Sadducees and the Pharisees began to argue, and the council split into two groups. The Sadducees didn't believe anyone was going to rise from the dead. They didn't believe in angels or spirits either. The Pharisees believed in all these things.

A great argument broke out, and the shouting became louder. Some of the Pharisees jumped up and argued violently, "We find nothing wrong with this man! Perhaps an angel or a spirit really did speak to him."

They became so violent, Lysias was afraid they would tear Paul to pieces between them. He ordered his soldiers to rescue Paul and take him back to the fortress.

That night the Lord appeared to Paul. "Be brave!" he said. "As you have boldly witnessed for me in Jerusalem, so you must give your witness for me in Rome."

20

Paul Witnesses to Rulers

Acts 23—26

PAUL'S enemies were determined to kill him. Early the next morning about forty of them met together secretly. They vowed that they wouldn't eat or drink until they had killed Paul. Then they went to the chief priests and elders.

"We've made a vow not to eat until we've killed Paul," they said. "Now you must make Lysias bring Paul to you. Pretend you want to question him some more. We'll be standing by ready to kill him before he gets here."

Paul's nephew heard about the plot, and he

went to the fortress and told Paul.

Paul called one of the officers. "Take this young man to Commander Lysias," he said. "He has something to tell him."

The officer took Paul's nephew to Lysias and said, "The prisoner Paul asked me to bring this young man to you. He has something to tell you."

Lysias took the young man by the hand and led him to a place where they wouldn't be overheard. "What do you have to tell me?" he asked.

"The Jewish leaders are plotting against Paul," Paul's nephew answered. "They're going to ask you to bring him to the council tomorrow. They'll pretend they want to ask him some more questions. But I beg you! Don't listen to them. More than forty men will be hiding and waiting for Paul. They've vowed not to eat or drink until they've killed him."

Lysias sent the young man away, warning him, "Don't tell a single soul that you've spoken to me."

Then Lysias called two of his officers and said, "Get two hundred men ready to go to Caesarea, along with seventy horsemen and two hundred spearmen. Have them ready to leave by nine o'clock tonight. Have horses ready to carry Paul safely to Governor Felix."

Then Commander Lysias wrote a letter to Antonius Felix, the Roman governor of Palestine, whose headquarters were at Caesarea. Lysias told Felix about Paul, and how he had decided to order Paul's enemies to make their charges in front of Felix.

The soldiers took Paul to Governor Felix, and Felix read Lysias' letter.

Felix spoke briefly to Paul, saying, "I'll hear your case when your accusers arrive." Then he ordered his men to keep Paul under guard.

Five days later the high priest and other leaders arrived in Caesarea with a lawyer named Tertullus. They made their accusations against Paul in front of Felix, as Lysias had ordered. Tertullus accused Paul of being a dangerous man.

"He starts riots among the Jews all over the world!" he said. "He's the ringleader of the Nazarenes. He was going to bring Gentiles into the temple when we arrested him. Question him and see for yourself. We're speaking the truth!"

The religious leaders joined in, accusing Paul and agreeing with Tertullus.

Paul answered, "I haven't broken the Jewish law. I didn't stir up trouble at the temple. They can't prove these charges. But I admit this: I worship the God of our ancestors in the way they say is false. At the same time, I believe everything that is written in the Jewish Scriptures. I have the same hope in God that they do—the hope that all people, good and bad, will rise from the dead."

When Paul was finished speaking, Felix said, "I'll give you my decision when Commander Lysias arrives."

Paul's enemies went back to Jerusalem, and Paul was put under guard.

A few days later Felix sent for Paul to come and speak to him and his wife, Drusilla, who was Jewish. Felix listened while Paul spoke about faith in Jesus Christ. But when Paul began to talk about justice and God's judgment, Felix became nervous.

"You can go now," he said to Paul. "I'll send for you again later."

This went on for two years. Felix kept sending for Paul to come and talk to him, but he never gave a decision about the accusations against Paul. Secretly, Felix was hoping that Paul would give him some money. He also wanted to impress the Jewish leaders, so he kept Paul a prisoner.

Then Felix was replaced by Porcius Festus, a new governor. Festus was under pressure from the Jewish leaders to send Paul back to Jerusalem.

He asked Paul if he would be willing to return to Jerusalem for a new trial. "I'll be in charge," Festus promised. He knew Paul didn't trust the Jewish council.

"I'm in a Roman court now," answered Paul. "That's where I belong. I've done nothing against Jewish law or the temple. Those charges they're making against me aren't true!"

Paul knew that Festus wanted to impress the Jewish leaders, and he said, "I'm not going to let you use me to win their favor. *I appeal to the emperor!*"

As a Roman citizen Paul had the right to a trial in the emperor's court. He knew this was the only way he could stop Festus from forcing him to return to Jerusalem and certain death.

Festus checked with his advisers and then he said to Paul, "You've appealed to the emperor, so to the emperor you will go!"

A few days later King Agrippa II, son of King Herod Agrippa I, came to Caesarea with his sister Bernice. Festus told them about Paul's case.

"When I heard the charges against Paul," he said, "I knew they didn't have a case. They were just arguing about their religion, and about a man named Jesus who died and Paul says is still alive. I don't know much about things like that, so I asked Paul to return to Jerusalem. But he refused. Instead, he appealed to the emperor. He's here under guard until I send him to Rome."

Agrippa was curious. "I'd like to hear this man myself," he said.

The next day Agrippa and Bernice and all their followers arrived, along with the important men of the city. Paul was brought in before them, tied with chains to the wrist of a Roman soldier.

Festus introduced Paul, and then he said, "I've decided to send him to Rome, but I need your help in preparing my report. We Romans aren't experts in Jewish law. I'd especially like you, King Agrippa, to question him."

King Agrippa said to Paul, "You have my permission to tell us your side of the story."

Paul began by telling them about his early life, and how he had become a believer. "I'm on trial because I have hope in the promise God made to our ancestors. Why can't you believe that God raises the dead? Here I stand as a witness. I say only what the prophets told would happen—that the Messiah would die and be the first to rise from the dead, that the Messiah would announce the message of light to both Jews and Gentiles!"

When Paul finished speaking, Festus shouted, "Paul, you're crazy! All your education has driven you out of your mind!"

"I'm not crazy, most noble Festus," answered

Paul. "I speak only the plain truth. The king understands these things." Then Paul said to King Agrippa, "King Agrippa, do you believe the prophets? But of course you do."

Agrippa answered, "Much more of this, Paul, and you'll be making me a Christian!"

"Oh," said Paul, "I just wish that you and everyone else here could stand in my place—but without these chains!"

Then the king stood up, and so did Festus and Bernice and all the other important people.

Outside they spoke about the case among themselves.

"This man doesn't deserve the death sentence," they agreed. "He shouldn't be a prisoner."

Then Agrippa said to Festus, "The man could easily have been set free—if only he hadn't appealed to the emperor!"

21

Shipwreck!

Acts 27

THE officials at Caesarea turned Paul and some other prisoners over to a Roman officer named Julius, to take them to Rome. Paul's friends Luke and Aristarchus went with him.

Julius took them by ship to Myra, on the southern coast of Asia Minor. On the way they stopped at Sidon, and Julius kindly allowed Paul to visit some friends there.

When they reached Myra, Julius found a large ship full of wheat from Alexandria, one of the last ships of the season to be sailing to Rome. It was late autumn, and all sea travel stopped in the winter.

Julius transferred Paul and the others onto the wheat ship. As they sailed from Myra, they met a strong northwest wind. They struggled against this wind for two weeks and finally reached the port of Cnidus. The wind was still blowing against them, so they turned south and sailed down the coast of Crete.

Everyone on the ship could see that they were in trouble. The ship struggled into the harbor of Fair Havens, where they waited for the wind to change.

Julius and the captain argued about whether to stay at Fair Havens or sail to Phoenix, a better port about fifty miles away.

Paul was an experienced sea traveler, so he gave them his advice. "Friends," he said, "I can see that the voyage to Phoenix will be dangerous. We might lose everything—not just the ship and the cargo, but even our lives!"

But the others didn't agree with Paul. Instead, they left Fair Havens. The weather was good, and they thought they would be safe. But soon the danger that Paul had warned about swept over them.

A terrible storm suddenly blew from across the island of Crete. A great wind hit the ship, making it impossible for them to stay on their course. They were driven away from Crete into the open sea.

They came to the little island of Clauda, and while they sailed near it, they were able to strengthen the ship against the storm. They pulled in the longboat that they had been towing behind them, and they fastened some rope around the ship.

The wind was so fierce, they were afraid they would be blown onto the sandbanks of North Africa, so they lowered the sails. This slowed the ship, and they drifted at the mercy of the storm.

The storm continued the next day. They threw some cargo overboard to lighten the ship. The third day they threw out some of the ship's equipment. Then they settled down to wait and hope.

The storm raged on and on day after day. They couldn't see the sun or the stars. They grew weak from hunger and lack of sleep. Finally, they gave up all hope of being saved. They waited for death.

But Paul never gave up hope. He went among the crew and passengers, comforting them.

"Friends," he said, "you should have listened to me. You shouldn't have sailed from Crete. If we had stayed at Fair Havens, we wouldn't be suffering now. But now I beg you—don't give up! None of you will die. Only the ship will be lost. I know this for certain, because last night an angel of my God stood by me and said, 'Don't be afraid, Paul. You must appear before the emperor. For this reason, God has spared the lives of everyone who is sailing with you.'

"Be brave, friends! I believe God. I'm sure everything will happen exactly as the angel told me. But we're going to have to run the ship aground on some island."

Finally, on the fourteenth night of the storm, they came near land. They were being driven back and forth in the sea between Italy and Sicily when suddenly the sailors felt there was land nearby. It was about midnight.

They measured the depth of the water by dropping a line. It was a hundred and twenty feet deep. After sailing a little farther, they dropped another line. The water was only ninety feet deep—a sure sign that they were coming close to land.

If they kept on moving so fast, they could crash on some rocks, so the sailors threw out four anchors and prayed for daylight. They could hear the sound of the waves hitting against a shore, but it was so dark, they didn't know where they were.

In the darkness the sailors plotted to escape from the ship before it crashed. They lowered the longboat into the water, pretending they were putting out some more anchors.

But Paul found out what they were doing. He said to Julius, "If these sailors don't stay on board the ship, there's no hope for the rest of you to be saved."

Julius ordered his soldiers to cut the ropes and let the longboat drop into the sea and drift away.

Then, while everyone waited for morning, Paul comforted them and encouraged them to eat.

"You've had nothing to eat for fourteen days," he said. "You haven't taken a bite the whole time you've been fighting the storm. I beg you, eat something! You have to, if you're going to survive. Believe me, not a hair of your heads will be lost!"

Paul took some bread and gave thanks to God right there in front of them. Then he broke it and began to eat. This made everyone feel so good, they ate, too. When they were full, they threw the wheat overboard to lighten the ship.

Daylight came, and they saw that they were anchored near a rocky island, with waves pounding against the shore. No one recognized the place, but they could see a bay and a sandy shore.

They decided to run the ship onto the soft ground. They cut away the anchors and let them sink into the sea. They cut the ropes that held the steering oars. Then they raised the front sail, so it would catch the wind, and headed for the sandy beach.

The ship struck some sand and the front became stuck. Then the waves began to hit the back of the ship and break it into pieces.

The soldiers were afraid the prisoners would escape, so they took out their swords, to kill them. Julius wanted to save Paul, so he stopped them. He gave orders for everyone who could swim to jump overboard and head for land while the rest followed, hanging onto pieces of the wrecked ship.

And so Paul and all the people who were sailing with him reached the shore safely, just as God had promised.

22

To the Ends
of the Earth

Acts 28; Philippians; Colossians;
Ephesians; Philemon; Titus; 1 and 2 Timothy

PAUL and his friends were shipwrecked on the island of Malta. When they were all safely ashore, the natives came down to welcome them. It was cold and raining, so they lit a big fire. Paul gathered a bundle of sticks to put on the fire. As he did, a snake came out of the fire and fastened itself to his hand.

"This man must be a murderer!" the natives said to each other. "He has escaped from the sea, but the goddess of Fate will kill him with that snake!"

Paul shook the snake off into the fire without being hurt. The natives expected him to swell up or drop dead, but after waiting a long time and seeing nothing happen to him, they changed their minds. They decided he was a god.

In that part of the island much of the land belonged to Publius, the Roman governor. He welcomed the crew and passengers from the shipwreck, and for three days they were his guests.

Now Publius' father happened to be in bed, sick with fever and diarrhea. Paul went to him and prayed for him. He laid his hands on him and healed him.

After that, all the sick people on the island

came to Paul to be healed. They loaded him and his friends with presents, and when the time came for them to leave, they gave them everything they needed for the voyage to Rome.

Three months later, in early spring, they sailed away on a wheat ship which had spent the winter at Malta. They reached the city of Syracuse on the island of Sicily and stayed there for three days. Then they sailed up the coast of Italy to Rhegium and Puteoli.

At Puteoli Paul and his friends found some believers. They stayed with them for a week. While they were there, the church in Rome heard that they had arrived and came to meet them.

When Paul saw them, he thanked God. He felt happy and excited. They traveled together to Rome on the Roman road called the Appian Way.

When they arrived at the imperial city, Paul was allowed to live in a house, instead of a prison, but a soldier was put on duty to guard him.

On his third day in Rome Paul invited the Jewish leaders to meet him. They came, and he told them about his arrest and his appeal to the emperor. "I wanted to let you know that I'm here in chains because of the hope of Israel," he said.

"We haven't heard anything about you," they answered. "Not from Judea or our people in Rome. We'd like to hear what you have to say, because everyone's talking against this religion of yours."

A few days later they returned with a large

number of their people. From morning until evening Paul spoke to them about the kingdom of God. He told them about his own faith and tried to show that the Jewish Scriptures proved that they should believe in Jesus.

Some of them believed, but others refused. When they couldn't all agree, they began to leave. As they were going, Paul said to them, "The Holy Spirit was right when he said to your ancestors, through the prophet Isaiah:

You will hear and not understand;
You will look and not see.

For your minds are slow,
    your ears are dull,
        and your eyes are closed.

If you would look with your eyes,
    listen with your ears,
        and think with your minds,

You would turn to God,
    and he would heal you.

"Understand this," said Paul. "This message of God's salvation has been sent to the Gentiles. At least they will listen!"

For the next two years Paul was a prisoner in his own house. Many of his friends came to visit him, and he spoke to everyone he met about Jesus.

Luke and John Mark and the believers from Asia, Achaia, and Macedonia brought news and letters from the churches, and Paul sent letters back to them. In his letters Paul taught the believers more about living as Christians.

He wrote to the Philippians about his joy in the Lord. "I want you to know that what has happened to me has turned out to be good for the gospel," he said. "Here in prison I can witness to the guards and everyone who comes and goes. Other Christians are encouraged by my example."

Paul wrote to the Colossians and the Ephesians, teaching them about the faith. Jesus is the bridge between Jews and Gentiles, he wrote. The church is the new family of God.

A Christian in Colossae had a slave named Onesimus who ran away. Paul helped Onesimus become a believer. Then he sent him back to his master, along with a letter to Philemon. In the letter Paul urged Philemon to treat his slave like a brother in Christ.

Timothy was working with the church in Ephesus, and Titus was building a new fellowship in Crete. Paul wrote to them, encouraging them in their work as church leaders.

Paul realized that his own time was nearly up. While he was in Rome, a great fire broke out, and Emperor Nero blamed it on the Christians. Nero began to persecute the church, and many believers were killed. Paul knew that he was going to die soon.

Before he was killed, Paul wrote to Timothy,

"As for me, I feel that the last drops of my life are being poured out for God. I have fought the fight that God gave me. I have finished the race. I have kept the faith."

23

Messages of Wisdom and Hope

Hebrews; Jude; James; 1 and 2 Peter; 1, 2, and 3 John

AFTER Paul's death a terrible time of persecution came upon the church. The Roman government turned against the Christians and cruelly persecuted them. At the same time, they sent an army to Jerusalem to put down a rebellion, and they completely destroyed the city.

Just as Jesus had foretold many years before, the temple was burned down and the people were scattered.

After the fall of Jerusalem, feelings between Jews and Christians grew bitter. The Jewish

133

leaders threw the Christians out of the synagogues, and the church became more Gentile than Jewish.

It was a difficult time for new believers. Some of them were so confused, they followed false teachers. Others copied the wicked behavior of the pagans around them.

In these times of persecution and hardship, James, Jude, Peter, John, and other church leaders wrote letters to give wisdom and hope to the believers. Peter and Paul were killed before the fall of Jerusalem, but some of the other apostles lived through that time. New leaders appeared, and the churches kept growing.

These letters to the churches were copied and

passed around and read out loud in each community. Later they were collected along with other writings and became part of the Christian Scriptures (the New Testament).

The believers learned from the letters how God still loved the Jewish people and how he wanted his new people, the church, to live and worship. They were encouraged to keep the faith, to do good deeds, and to be kind to each other.

Here are some of the teachings they learned from the letters of the apostles:

Faith means trusting in the things we hope for. Faith means being sure of things we cannot see.

Faith without action is dead.

Be glad when you are tested by persecution. When that happens, you are sharing the sufferings of Christ. After that you will be filled with joy.

Let us keep on loving one another, because love comes from God. Everyone who really loves God is a child of God and understands what God is like.

We know that God loves us because he sent his only Son into the world to give us life through him. If God loves us that much, surely we can love one another!

We love God because God first loved us. If we say we love God but hate our brother, we are liars. If we don't love the brother we can see, how can we love the God we cannot see?

You will suffer, but then God himself will make you whole and safe and strong. All power belongs to God, forever and ever.

God Makes
All Things New

John's Letter to the Seven Churches

Revelation 1—3

DURING the time when the Romans were persecuting the church, a leader named John was sent to the island of Patmos, in the Aegean Sea near Ephesus. John was a prisoner because he had witnessed to Jesus.

One day on the first day of the week, the Holy Spirit fell on John, and he saw a strange and wonderful vision. He heard a voice as loud as a trumpet calling to him.

"Write down everything you see," said the voice. "Write it in a book, and send the book to the seven churches in the cities of Ephesus,

Smyrna, Pergamum, Thyatira, Sardis, Philadelphia, and Laodicea."

John turned around to see who was speaking to him. He saw seven golden lampstands, and among the lampstands he saw someone who looked like a human being.

The person in John's vision was dressed in a long robe with a golden belt tied at his waist. His hair was as white as snow, and his eyes blazed like fire. His feet were shining like polished bronze. His voice sounded like a roaring waterfall. In his right hand he held seven stars. A sharp two-edged sword came out of his mouth, and his face was as bright as the noonday sun.

When John saw this person, this Son of Man, he fell down at his feet like a dead man. John was filled with holy fear, because the person in his vision was the risen Lord Jesus Christ.

"Don't be afraid!" said Jesus, and he touched John with his right hand. "I am the first and the last, the living one. I was dead, but now I am alive forever and ever. I hold in my hand the keys of death and the grave.

"Write down everything you see. Some of the things in this vision are happening now, and some will happen in the future. See the seven stars in my right hand and the seven lampstands. Here is their secret meaning: the seven stars are the angels of the seven churches, and the seven lampstands are the churches."

Then in the vision Jesus told John to send a

message to each of the seven churches.

"Write to the angel of the church in Ephesus: 'This is the message of the one who holds the seven stars safe in his right hand, the one who walks among the seven lampstands:

" 'I know all about you. I know how hard you have worked. You are patient in your suffering. Yet I have this complaint about you: you don't love me now as much as you did at first. Turn back to living as you used to, or I'll take away your lampstand. You have this in your favor: you hate false teaching as much as I do.

" 'Let everyone who has ears to hear pay attention to what the Spirit is saying to the churches! To those who win the victory I will give the right to eat from the tree of life that grows in the garden of God.'

"Next, write to the angel of the church in Smyrna: 'This is the message of the one who is the first and the last, the one who died and came to life again:

" 'I know about your troubles and your poverty. But you have true riches! I know what evil things false believers are saying about you. Don't be afraid. You will suffer and your faith will be tested, but your suffering will pass. Be faithful, and I will give you the crown of life.

" 'Let everyone who has ears to hear pay attention to what the Spirit is saying to the churches! Those who win the victory cannot be hurt by the second death.'

"Now write this to the angel of the church in Pergamum: 'This is the message of the one who has the sharp two-edged sword:

" 'I know that you live in an evil place. I know that you are faithful. Yet I have this complaint about you: some of you follow false teachers. Turn from this sin, or I'll attack you with the sword that comes out of my mouth.

" 'Let everyone who has ears to hear pay attention to what the Spirit is saying to the churches! To those who win the victory I will give the hidden bread from heaven. I will also give them a white stone with a new name written on it—a name that nobody will know except the person who receives it.'

"Write this to the angel of the church in Thyatira: 'This is the message of the Son of God, whose eyes blaze like fire and whose feet shine like polished bronze:

" 'I know all about you. I know that you are kind and loyal. You serve patiently, and you are doing more now than you did at first. Yet I have this complaint about you: you encourage false teaching. I will punish the false prophet and her followers. To the rest of you, I say, "Hold on to what you have until I come."

" 'To those who win the victory, I will give power over the nations. I will give them the morning star. Let everyone who has ears to hear pay attention to what the Spirit is saying to the churches!'

"Write this to the angel of the church in Sardis: 'This is the message of the one who holds in his hand the seven angels of God and the seven stars:

" 'I know all about you. You seem to be alive, but you are really dead. Wake up! Strengthen what you have before it's too late. Go back to what you were when you first heard the message. If you refuse to wake up, I'll come like a thief when you don't expect me. Yet some of you have stayed pure. You will walk with me, dressed in white, as you deserve.

" 'Those who win the victory will wear white robes. I will never erase their names from the book of life. I will speak their names openly in the presence of my Father and his angels. Let everyone who has ears to hear pay attention to what the Spirit is saying to the churches!'

"Now write to the angel of the church in Philadelphia: 'This is the message of the holy and true one. He holds the key that can open any door so nobody can shut it. When he shuts a door, nobody can open it.

" 'I know all about you. You aren't very strong, but you have faithfully followed my teachings. I have opened a door for you which nobody can shut. Because you have been faithful, I will watch over you during the time of trouble that is coming upon the whole world. I am coming soon. Hold on tight to what you have. Don't let anyone take away your crown of victory.

" 'Those who win the victory I will make pillars in the temple of my God, and they will never leave it. I will write on them the name of my God, and the name of the city of my God—the new Jerusalem—which comes down out of heaven from my God. I will write my own new name on them. Let everyone who has ears to hear pay attention to what the Spirit is saying to the churches!'

"Finally, write to the angel of the church in Laodicea: 'This is the message of the Amen, the faithful and true witness, the beginning of God's creation:

" 'I know all about you. You are neither hot nor cold. I wish you were hot or cold, but since you are lukewarm, I will spit you out of my mouth.

You say you are rich, but you are really poor and blind and naked. If you want to be really rich, buy true gold from me. Take white robes from me to cover your nakedness, and eye ointment to cure your blindness. See! I stand at the door and knock. If anyone hears my voice and opens the door, I will go into his house and eat with him, and he will eat with me.

" 'To those who win the victory I will give the honor of sitting next to me on my throne, just as I have won the victory and now I sit beside my Father on his throne. Let everyone who has ears to hear pay attention to what the Spirit is saying to the churches!' "

25

The Throne of God

Revelation 4—5

AFTER he saw the vision of Jesus, and heard the letters to the seven churches, John saw another vision. He saw a door standing open in heaven, and he heard the same voice, the voice that sounded like a trumpet.

"Come up here," said the voice. "I will show you what is going to happen in the future."

Immediately John felt the Spirit inspiring him. In his vision he saw a throne set up in heaven, and someone was sitting on it. The one sitting on the throne was shining like diamonds. All around the throne was a circle of light like an emerald rainbow. Around the throne were twenty-four other thrones. Sitting on these thrones were twenty-four elders. They were dressed in white robes and wearing golden crowns on their heads.

From the throne in the middle came flashes of lightning and loud noises and the rumbling of thunder. Seven lamps burned in front of the throne—they were the seven angels of God. In front of the throne was a sea of glass. It was as clear as crystal.

Around the throne were four living creatures, covered in front and back with eyes. The first creature looked like a lion, the second like a bull, the third had a human face, and the fourth looked like a flying eagle. Each of the creatures had six wings, and they were completely covered with eyes inside and out.

Day and night the four creatures sang without stopping:

> Holy, holy, holy
> is the Lord God Almighty,
>
> Who was, and is,
> and is coming.

The living creatures kept giving glory and honor and thanksgiving to the one who sat on the throne—the one who lives forever and ever. At the same time the twenty-four elders bowed down before the one on the throne and worshiped him, the one who lives forever and ever. They threw their crowns in front of the throne and sang:

> You are worthy,
>   O Lord our God,
>   to receive glory and honor and power,
>   Because you created all things.
>   By your will
>   everything was created.

John saw a book in the right hand of the one sitting on the throne. It was a scroll with writing all over it, front and back, and it was sealed with seven seals.

Then John saw a mighty angel, and the angel called out in a loud voice, "Who is worthy to open the book and break the seven seals?"

Nobody in heaven or on earth or under the earth was able to open the book, or even to look at it. John began to cry because there was nobody worthy to open the book or even look at it.

Then one of the twenty-four elders said to John, "Don't cry. Look! The lion from the tribe of Judah has won the victory. He is able to open the book and break the seven seals."

John looked at the throne and saw someone standing in the very center—a Lamb who looked as if he had been killed. The Lamb had seven horns and seven eyes, so he could see everything that happens on the earth. While John was watching, the Lamb came and took the scroll

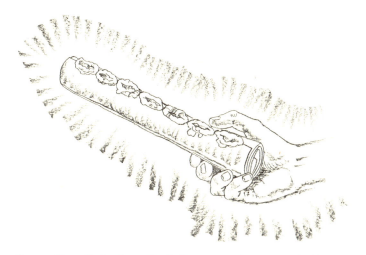

from the right hand of the one who was sitting on the throne.

Then the four living creatures and the twenty-four elders bowed down in front of the Lamb. Each of them had a harp and a golden bowl full of incense. This incense was the prayers of the saints. Together the creatures and the elders sang a new song, a song of praise to the Lamb:

> You are worthy to take the book
> and break open its seals,
>   for you have been killed.
>
> And with your blood you have bought
>   for God
>
> People from every tribe and language
>   and nation and race.
>
> You have made them a kingdom of priests
>   to serve our God,

And they will rule as kings
upon the earth!

In his vision John heard the voices of thousands of angels circling around the throne and the creatures and the elders. There were tens of thousands of them, a thousand times a thousand. Together they all sang:

Worthy is the Lamb who was killed!
He is worthy to receive
power and riches
and wisdom and strength
and honor and glory and praise!

Then John heard the voice of every living creature in heaven and on the earth and under the earth and on the sea. They were all singing together:

Let us give
praise and honor,
glory and power

To the one who sits on the throne
and to the Lamb
Forever and ever!

"Amen!" said the four living creatures, and the elders fell down and worshiped.

26

The Lamb Breaks the Seven Seals

Revelation 6—7

WHILE John watched, the Lamb broke the seven seals one by one. Each time a seal was broken, something terrible appeared.

When the Lamb broke the first seal, John heard one of the four creatures shout in a voice like thunder, "Come out!"

A white horse appeared, with a rider. The rider carried a bow, and he was given a crown of victory. He rode out to conquer and win battles.

When the Lamb broke the second seal, John heard the second creature shout, "Come out!"

A red horse appeared. Its rider was given power to take peace from the earth. A huge sword of war was put in his hand.

When the Lamb broke the third seal, John heard the third creature shout, "Come out!"

A black horse appeared. Its rider held a pair of scales in his hand. John heard a voice saying, "Food is scarce! Measure the wheat and barley!"

The Lamb broke the fourth seal, and John heard the voice of the fourth creature shout, "Come out!"

A pale horse appeared. The rider of the pale horse was named Death, and the grave followed close behind him, to swallow up his victims. One fourth of the earth was put into their power, to be killed by the sword, by hunger, by disease, and by wild beasts.

Then John saw the Lamb break the fifth seal, and he heard the souls of the people who had been killed for witnessing to God's message. These martyrs were crying, "How long will it be, holy and true Lord? When will you judge the people of the earth and punish them for killing us?"

Each of these souls received a white robe. They were told to wait a little while longer, until the rest of the martyrs were killed.

When the Lamb broke the sixth seal, there was a violent earthquake, and the sun turned black. The moon turned red and the stars fell down from the sky. Then the sky disappeared, like a

scroll being rolled up, and every mountain and island was removed.

The kings of the earth and the great men, the generals and the rich and powerful men, and everyone, slave and free, ran to the hills and hid in caves and among the rocks. They cried out to the mountains and the rocks, "Fall on us and hide us from the one who sits on the throne, and from the Lamb's anger! The great day of their anger is here. Who can stand up against it?"

Then John saw four angels standing at the four corners of the earth. They were holding the four winds to keep them from blowing over the land or the sea or on the trees.

Another angel came up from the east, carrying

the seal of the living God. "Wait!" he called to the four angels who held back the winds. "Don't hurt the earth or the sea or the trees until we have put a mark on the foreheads of God's servants."

They marked 144,000 people with God's seal—12,000 people from each of the twelve tribes of Israel.

Then John saw an enormous crowd from every nation and tribe, people of every race and language. They were standing in front of the throne and in front of the Lamb. They were dressed in white robes, and in their hands they held palm branches.

With a great voice the whole crowd shouted, "Victory to our God, who sits on the throne! Victory to the Lamb!"

All the angels who were standing in a circle around the throne bowed down and worshiped God. "Amen!" they said.

> Praise and glory
>   and wisdom and thanksgiving,
>
> Honor and power and might
>   belong to our God
>
> Forever and ever!

Then one of the elders came up to John and asked, "Who are these people dressed in white robes? Where do they come from?"

"I don't know, sir," answered John. "Tell me."

"These are the martyrs," explained the elder. "They have been through the great persecution. They have washed their robes in the blood of the Lamb. That is why they now stand in front of God's throne and worship him day and night in his temple. He will take care of them. They will never be hungry or thirsty again. The sun and the wind won't bother them. For the Lamb will be their shepherd, and he will lead them to springs of living water. God will wipe away every tear from their eyes."

27

Visions of Seven Disasters

Revelation 8—11

THE Lamb broke the seventh seal, and there was silence in heaven for about half an hour.

Then John saw an angel standing by the golden altar that was in front of God's throne. The angel was holding a golden pan of incense. These were the prayers of the saints, and he offered them on the altar. The smoke of the burning incense rose up before God.

The prayers of the saints brought on the great day of God's anger. The angel took the golden pan and filled it with fire from the altar and threw it down onto the earth. Then there were thunder and flashes of lightning and an earthquake.

John saw seven angels with seven trumpets. As each one blew his trumpet, a terrible disaster came upon the earth.

First hail and fire mixed with blood came pouring down, and then a great fiery mountain was thrown into the sea. A huge star fell from the sky, blazing like a torch, and the light of the sun and moon and stars grew dim.

Monsters like grasshoppers came charging into battle, and a great army led by fallen angels attacked the people of the earth.

After the sixth disaster struck, another mighty angel came down from heaven, wrapped in a cloud, with a rainbow around his head. His face was shining like the sun, and his legs were like pillars of fire. In his hand he held a little open book. The angel put his right foot on the sea and his left foot on the land, and he shouted with a voice like a lion's roar. Seven booms of thunder answered him.

John was writing down everything he saw and heard, but then a voice from heaven told him, "What the thunder said is a secret. Don't write it down."

Then the mighty angel raised his right hand to heaven and said, "The time of waiting is over! When the seventh angel blows his trumpet, God's secret plan will be complete, just as he promised

long ago through his prophets."

The voice from heaven spoke to John again, saying, "Go and take the little book from the angel's hand."

John went to the angel and asked him for the book.

"Take it and eat it," said the angel. "It will be bitter in your stomach, but it will taste as sweet as honey in your mouth."

John took the little book and swallowed it. It tasted as sweet as honey in his mouth, but it was bitter in his stomach.

John was told to speak God's message to the people of the world, and he was given a rod to measure the temple and the altar. He heard about two witnesses who would speak God's message, and then he saw the last disaster.

The seventh angel blew his trumpet and loud voices in heaven called out:

> The kingdom of the world
>   has now become
> The kingdom of our Lord and his Christ.

> And he will reign forever and ever!

The twenty-four elders fell down and worshiped God, saying, "We give thanks to you, Lord God Almighty, who is and who was. We thank you for using your great power and beginning your reign."

Then came the time for God's anger: the time to judge the dead, the time to reward God's servants, and the time to destroy the people who destroy the earth.

28

The Woman, the Dragon, and the Beast

Revelation 11—14

GOD'S heavenly temple was opened, and John could see inside. Lightning flashed, thunder roared, and there was a great earthquake and a violent hailstorm.

A huge figure appeared in the sky. It was a woman who was clothed in the sun. The moon was under her feet, and on her head was a crown of twelve stars. She was crying out as she gave birth to a baby.

Then a second figure appeared in the sky. This was a huge red dragon with seven heads and ten

horns. He had a crown on each of his heads. The
dragon's tail knocked some stars from the sky
and threw them down to earth.

The dragon stood in front of the woman, waiting for her child to be born so he could eat it. But
the child was snatched from the dragon and
taken up to God. (The child was the Son of God
who will rule the nations.)

Meanwhile, the woman escaped to the wilderness, to a place that God had prepared for her.

Then war broke out in heaven. Michael and his
angels fought against the dragon and his angels,
and the dragon was defeated. The huge dragon,
who is also called the devil or Satan, was thrown
down to earth, and his angels with him.

A voice shouted from heaven, "Now is the victory of the kingdom of our God! Christ has all power, and Satan has been thrown out of heaven! Let the heavens be glad! But how terrible it will be for the earth, for Satan is filled with rage, because he knows that his time is short."

As soon as the dragon realized where he was, he began to chase the woman. She received two eagles' wings to fly to a safe place in the wilderness. When she escaped, the dragon was so angry, he attacked the rest of the woman's children. (These are the people who obey God and witness to Jesus.)

In his vision John was standing on the seashore and he saw a beast come up from the sea. It had seven heads and ten horns. On each of its seven heads were names that insulted God. The beast looked like a leopard with bear's feet and a lion's mouth.

The dragon gave the beast his own power and the power to rule the world. The whole world was impressed with the beast. Everyone worshiped the dragon because he had given his power to the beast.

"Who is like the beast?" they asked. "Who could ever defeat it?"

The beast was allowed to brag and insult God and do whatever it wanted for three and a half years. It spoke against God and his temple and everyone who lived in heaven. It was allowed to attack and conquer the saints. It was given power over people from every tribe and nation, people of every race and language.

Everyone on earth worshiped the beast— everyone except the people whose names were written in the Lamb's book of life.

Then a second beast came up out of the earth. It had two horns like a lamb, but it made noises like a dragon. This second beast was the servant of the first beast. It was a false prophet who forced everyone to worship the first beast. It did great miracles and impressed everyone on earth.

The second beast convinced the people to make a statue in honor of the first beast. Then it breathed life into the statue so it could speak, and it put to death anyone who refused to worship it.

Next the first beast forced everyone on earth to receive a mark on their right hands or their foreheads. No one was allowed to buy or sell anything unless they had the mark of the name of the beast, or the number of its name. The number that stood for the name of the beast was 666.

After John saw the beast and its followers, he saw the Lamb and his followers. The Lamb was sitting on Mount Zion with 144,000 people who had the Lamb's name and his Father's name written on their foreheads.

Then a voice came from heaven. It sounded like the roar of the ocean or the music of harps. The 144,000 people were standing in front of God's throne, singing a new song of praise. These people were the only ones of the whole human race who had been saved. They had not worshiped idols, but they had followed the Lamb.

29

The Seven Last Punishments

Revelation 14—16

NEXT John saw an angel flying high in the air, carrying the message of salvation to everyone on earth.

"Honor God and praise him!" cried the angel. "The time has come for God to judge everyone on earth. Worship God, the Creator of heaven and earth and sea!"

A second angel followed the first one. "Babylon has fallen!" he cried. "The wicked city has been destroyed."

Then a third angel came, shouting, "Whoever

worships the beast and its statue, whoever receives the mark of the beast, will have to drink the wine of God's anger and be punished forever and ever."

A voice came from heaven, saying to John, "Write this down: Happy are the people who die while serving the Lord! They will rest from their work. Their good deeds will follow them."

Then John saw a white cloud with an angel sitting on it. The angel had a golden crown on his head and a sharp sickle in his hand.

Another angel came out of the heavenly temple and called to the angel on the cloud, "Take your sickle and reap the harvest. The time has come! The harvest of the earth is ripe!"

The angel swung his sickle over the earth, cutting the grapes from the vine. He threw the grapes into the great winepress of God's anger, and they were stamped on until blood flowed out like a river.

Then a great and terrible sign appeared in heaven: seven angels holding seven bowls. The bowls contained God's seven last punishments.

A sea of glass appeared, mixed with fire. Standing by the glassy sea were the people who had defeated the beast and its statue and the number of its name. These people were holding harps given to them by God. They were singing the song of Moses and the song of the Lamb:

Great and wonderful are your works,
O Lord God Almighty!

Right and true are you ways,
O King of the nations!

Who could refuse to honor you
and praise your name, O Lord?

Only you are holy!
All the nations will come and worship you,
for your justice is clear!

Then John saw seven angels coming out of the heavenly temple. They were dressed in pure white linen with golden belts tied around their waists. One of the four living creatures gave the seven angels the seven golden bowls filled with the anger of God. The temple was filled with smoke from the glory and power of God. No one could enter the temple until the seven punishments were poured out.

A loud voice from the temple said to the seven angels, "Go out and pour out upon the earth the seven bowls of God's anger!"

The first angel poured his bowl onto the earth, and sores broke out on the people who had the mark of the beast.

The second angel poured his bowl out into the sea. The sea turned to blood, and everything in the sea died.

The third angel emptied his bowl into the rivers and they turned to blood, punishing the people who spilled the blood of the saints and the prophets.

The fourth angel emptied his bowl over the sun, and the sun burned people with its heat. Still the people kept on insulting God and refusing to turn from their sins.

The fifth angel emptied his bowl over the throne of the beast. Darkness fell over the kingdom of the beast. Its people suffered great pain, but even so they refused to turn away from their sins.

The sixth angel poured his bowl over the great river Euphrates, and the river dried up, making a road for an invasion by the kings coming from the east.

Then three evil spirits that looked like frogs came out of the mouths of the dragon, the beast,

and the second beast that was a false prophet.
The evil spirits gathered together the kings of the
world to fight a battle on the great day of
Almighty God. They brought them to a place
called Armageddon.

30

The Last Battle

Revelation 16—20

THE seventh angel poured his bowl into the air, and a voice shouted from the temple, "The end has come!"

Lightning flashed and thunder roared. The worst earthquake in the history of the world shook the earth. Great cities were destroyed, and every island and mountain disappeared. Huge hailstones fell like heavy weights from the sky.

"Come!" said one of the seven angels to John. "I'll show you the punishment of the great city that is built beside many rivers. That city is like

a prostitute. It is a wicked woman who has led
the kings and the people of the world into terrible
sins."

The angel carried John away into the wilderness, where he saw a woman riding on a red
beast. The beast was covered with names that insulted God. It had seven heads and ten horns.

The woman was dressed in purple and scarlet.
She was glittering with gold and jewels and
pearls. In her hand she held a golden cup filled
with disgusting and evil things. On her forehead
was written: Babylon the great, mother of all the
prostitutes and perverts of the earth.

John saw that the woman was drunk with the
blood of the saints and the people who had been

killed for witnessing to Jesus. He was amazed by the sight of her.

"Why are you amazed?" asked the angel. "I'll tell you the secret meaning of this woman and the beast she's riding. The beast was once alive, but now it is dead. The seven heads are the seven hills of the great city, and the seven kings of the city. The beast is an eighth king. The ten horns are ten future kings.

"The kings will give their power to the beast. They will make war on the Lamb, but the Lamb and his faithful followers will defeat them, because the Lamb is Lord of lords and King of kings.

"In the future everyone will turn against the woman. They will take away everything she has and completely destroy her. All this is in God's plan, for the woman is the great city that rules over the kings of the earth."

John saw another angel coming down from heaven with great power and glory. "Babylon has fallen!" shouted the angel. "Babylon the Great has fallen! She is being punished in the same way she has caused others to suffer. Great is the Lord God, who is judging her!"

A voice from heaven spoke about Babylon's fall. The rulers of the earth cried over her, but in heaven God's people celebrated her fall. They sang:

Alleluia!
Victory and glory and power belong to our God!

He judges fairly;
he punishes rightly.

He has judged the wicked woman
 who was ruining the earth with her sin;
 she was killing God's people.

Alleluia!
The smoke from the burning city
 will rise up forever and ever!

The twenty-four elders and the four living creatures bowed down and worshiped God, singing, "Amen! Alleluia!"

Then from the heavenly throne came a voice, saying, "Praise God! Praise him, all his servants! Praise him, all people!"

A great crowd praised God. They sounded like a mighty waterfall or roaring thunder as they cried, "Alleluia! The rule of the Lord God has begun! His kingdom has come.

"Let us rejoice and be glad! Let us give him the glory.

"Now is the time for the wedding of the Lamb. His bride is ready. She is dressed in shining white linen, made from the good deeds of the saints."

Then the angel said to John, "Write this down: 'Happy are the people who are invited to the wedding party of the Lamb!' "

John started to worship the angel, and the angel said, "Don't do that! I'm a servant, like you and your friends. We are all witnesses to Jesus. Give your worship to God!"

Then John saw a vision of the last battle. Heaven opened, and a white horse appeared. Its rider was called Faithful and True, because he judges fairly and fights for justice. His eyes blazed like fire, and he wore many crowns on his head. He had a secret name written on him. His robe was soaked with blood. He was called the Word of God.

Behind him the armies of heaven rode on white horses. They were dressed in pure white linen.

From the rider's mouth came a sharp sword to strike the nations. On his robe and on his thigh was his name: King of kings and Lord of lords.

Then an angel shouted to the birds in the sky, "Come here and eat the flesh of kings and officers, the flesh of heroes and horses and riders— the flesh of the wicked!"

Then the beast appeared, along with all the kings of the earth and their armies. They had gathered together to fight against the rider and his army. The beast and the false prophet were taken prisoner, and both of them were thrown into the lake of fire. The rest were killed by the sword of the rider. When it was over, the birds of the sky came and ate their flesh.

Then John saw an angel coming down from heaven. The angel held the key to the pit and a heavy chain. He grabbed the dragon and chained him up for a thousand years. He threw the dragon into the pit and locked it and sealed it.

Next John saw some thrones with judges sitting on them. He saw the souls of the people who had been killed for witnessing for Jesus and the people who refused to bow down to the beast. These souls came to life, and they ruled with Christ for a thousand years.

The angel told John that after a thousand years the dragon, Satan, will be set free from the pit. He will try to fool the nations of the earth. He will lead an army into battle, surrounding the army of the saints. The saints will defend the city that God loves. Then fire will come down from heaven and destroy Satan's army. Satan will be thrown into the lake of fire, where he will join the beast and the false prophet. They will stay in the lake of fire forever and ever.

Then John saw a vision of the last judgment. He saw a great white throne, with someone sitting on it. Then heaven and earth disappeared. All the dead, both great and small, stood in front of the throne, and the books were opened. Then the book of life was opened, and the dead were judged according to what they had done, as it was written in the books.

Death and the grave were destroyed in the lake of fire. Anyone whose name was not written in the book of life was thrown into the lake.

In this way all evil was completely destroyed.

31

God Makes All Things New

Revelation 21—22

THEN John saw a new heaven and a new earth. The first heaven and the first earth had disappeared, and there was no more sea. He saw the holy city, the new Jerusalem, coming down from God out of heaven. The city was like a bride, beautifully dressed for her husband.

"Look!" said a great voice from the heavenly throne. "Now God's home is with his people, and he will stay with them. They will be his people, and he will be their God. He will wipe away every tear. Death will be no more. Never again will there be sadness or crying or pain. All those things are gone forever."

Then the one who was sitting on the throne said, *"Look! I am making all things new!"* He added, "Write this down, for my words are true." Then he said, "It is finished! I am everything from A to Z, the beginning and the end, the Alpha and the Omega. I will give water to the thirsty from the fountain of life. I will reward the faithful. I will be their God, and they will be my children. But sinners and idol-worshipers will be punished."

One of the seven angels who held the seven bowls went to John and said, "Come here and I will show you the bride of the Lamb."

The angel showed John a vision of the new Jerusalem. He carried John in the spirit to the top of a great mountain and John saw the holy city coming down out of heaven from God. The city was shining with the glory of God. It was glittering like a precious jewel.

A high wall surrounded the city. It had twelve gates, three on each side. At each gate stood an angel, and above the gates were written the names of the twelve tribes of Israel.

The city was a perfect square built on twelve great foundation stones. On each stone was written the name of one of the twelve apostles of the Lamb.

The angel measured the city with a golden measuring rod. It was twelve thousand measures

long, twelve thousand measures wide, and twelve thousand measures high.

The wall of the city was made of diamonds. The city itself was built of purest gold, as shiny as glass. The foundation stones were made from twelve different precious jewels. Each of the twelve gates was made from a single enormous pearl. The street was paved with pure gold.

There was no temple in the city, because the Lord God Almighty and the Lamb were the temple. The city didn't need the light of the sun or the moon, because the glory of God filled the city with light, and its glow was the Lamb.

In the future the nations will walk by the light of the city, and the rulers of the earth will bring their glory to it. The gates of the city will stand open day after day. There will be no night. The wealth of the nations will be brought to the city. Nothing unclean or wicked will be allowed to enter—only the people whose names are written in the Lamb's book of life.

Then the angel showed John the river of the water of life. It sparkled like crystal as it flowed from the throne of God and the Lamb. It ran down the middle of the street, and on each side of it grew the trees of life. On the trees grew a different kind of fruit each month, and the leaves of the trees gave healing medicine for all people.

In the future the throne of God and the Lamb will be in the city. The servants of God will worship him. They will see his face. His name will be written on their foreheads. The Lord will shine his light on them, and they will rule as kings forever and ever.

The heavenly vision ended, and the angel told John to write down everything he had seen and share it with the churches.

Jesus himself told John, "Listen! I am coming soon. I will reward the faithful and I will punish the wicked. The faithful will enter the holy city and eat from the tree of life. But the wicked will be locked out.

"I have sent my angel to you," said Jesus. "Take this message to the churches, for I have shown you these things for their sake."

John wrote down everything he saw in these

wonderful visions. He sent the message to the churches, as Jesus had commanded.

The believers were encouraged when they read about the wonderful things that had been shown to John. They felt strengthened to stand up and be faithful witnesses to Jesus. If they suffered, Jesus would reward them, and someday their enemies would be punished. Now they knew for sure that they had nothing to fear from the rich and powerful people who were persecuting them, because God would take care of them. God's kingdom was coming, and he would rule forever and ever.

They believed that Jesus was coming soon, in the clouds, and everyone on earth would see him.

Jesus promised, "I am coming soon."

His faithful followers answered, "Come, Lord Jesus."

THE WORLD OF PAUL

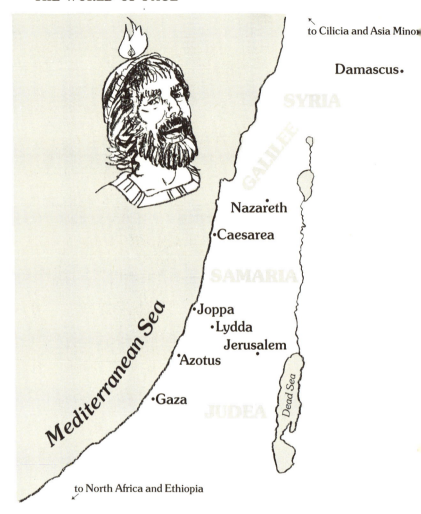

to Cilicia and Asia Minor

Damascus•

SYRIA

GALILEE

Nazareth

•Caesarea

SAMARIA

•Joppa

•Lydda

Jerusalem

•Azotus

•Gaza

JUDEA

Mediterranean Sea

Dead Sea

to North Africa and Ethiopia

THE WORLD OF THE EARLY CHURCH

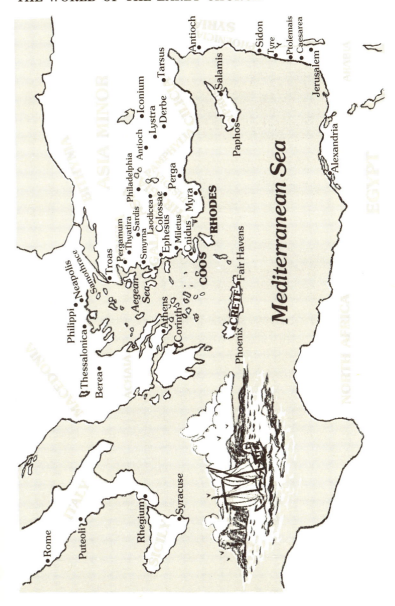

Eve Bowers MacMaster graduated from Pennsylvania State University and George Washington University. She also studied at Harvard University and Eastern Mennonite Seminary. She has taught in the Bible department at Eastern Mennonite College and in the history department at James Madison University, both located in Harrisonburg, Virginia.

Eve visited many of the places mentioned in the Bible while she was serving as a Peace Corps volunteer in Turkey.

Eve and her husband, Richard, live in Bluffton, Ohio, with their children, Sam, Tom, and Sarah.